# Glenwood Springs
## A Quick History

### INCLUDING GLENWOOD CANYON

**By Jim Nelson**

Cover illustration of the Hotel Colorado, Glenwood Springs, by Sam Thiewes



Published by Blue Chicken Publishing
1512 Grand Ave., Glenwood Springs, CO 81601

Printed in the United States

ISBN 1-928971-00-8

# Table of Contents

CHAPTER 1

# A LANDSCAPE THAT KEPT REARRANGING ITSELF

An incomprehensible number of years in the past, back in the shadowy days of the armored fish and the 50-foot shark, a vast inland sea covered much of what is now Colorado. Then, some 300 million years ago, the geological plates beneath the oceans buckled and cracked, forcing the broken edges many thousands of feet upwards. These rocks thrust into the open air, eventually forming enormous mountain ranges. Geologists estimate that they may have reached 25,000, perhaps even 35,000 feet into the air. This craggy expanse of rock formed the spine of what was to become the North American Continent. It would be easy to imagine that, given millions of years of scouring by wind and water, one set of those mountains was worn down to what we today call the Rockies. Well, things, as things tend to do, got a little out of hand.

Over time, lots of time, the mountains were indeed worn away. Almost completely. What had been majestic pinnacles were gradually reduced to grains of sand, to be washed relentlessly downstream. The sediment formed over the millennia spread itself over the high plains to the west of the mountains, and also covered what was to become Eastern Colorado, Nebraska, and Kansas. A great deal of the deposited material was a rusty red in color. It was the result of iron oxide contained in the rocks of what were to be known as the "Ancestral Rockies".

The existing continents were all once part of a huge land mass known as "Pangea". The supercontinent began breaking apart some 60 million years ago. North America separated from Europe and South America broke away from Africa; the resulting gap formed the Atlantic Ocean. During the same period, another major upheaval occurred in the area of the now stunted mountains, creating the basis for

*Caldera (center) of the Dotsero Volcano. Photo taken about 1921.* (Courtesy of Al Maggard)

the present Rockies. This massive upthrust formed the White River Plateau, a high, reasonably level area. At the same time, the pressure from beneath the plates cracked them in many places, allowing the molten rock which had formed well below the surface to surge upwards. The magma exploded into the air, further building up the layers of rock in the area. Dotsero, at the east end of the Glenwood Canyon, is the site of a long-extinct volcano. The cone is still visible, and Interstate 70 rises slightly as it passes over the ancient lava flow. The area around Dotsero is still littered with the dark, porous "lava rock", and the surrounding hills reveal the gray band of the resultant ash deposit.

Mount Sopris is the towering snow-capped peak that sits 15 miles to the south of Glenwood Springs, and visually fills the gap formed by the Roaring Fork Valley. It is an example of what is known as an igneous intrusion. It was formed from molten rock that forced its way upwards, elevating the overlying terrain. The rock that was pushed up by the intrusion has since eroded away, leaving the magnificent mountain of hardened igneous rock that we see today.

*Mount Sopris - volcanic "igneous intrusion."* (Courtesy of Scott Leslie)

Envision a giant layer cake. Each of the many hundreds of layers contains the geologic record, the memory, of a certain period of time. If you look at a slice of that huge cake, you would be looking at the fossil history of that area. Because of deposition, the depositing of sediment by wind and water, the remains of plants and animals and mineral deposits tend to be covered and therefore preserved for future viewing. We need only the opportunity to uncover the resultant layers. The uplifting of the Rockies brought about an obvious increase in the velocity of the flow of the streams and rivers that drain the vast snowfields of the high country. This increase in gradient allowed the rushing water to cut deeply into the rock, exposing the edges of increasingly older memories. In places deep within Glenwood Canyon, it is possible to see, and to touch, rock that began forming literally billions of years ago.

*Aerial view of Glenwood Canyon, some 2,000 feet deep.* (Courtesy of Frontier Historical Society)

Along Highway 82 south of Glenwood Springs, and in Glenwood Canyon to the east, you can see towering cliffs of the red sandstone that once washed down from the Ancestral Rockies. The alluvial fan, the curved north cliff of Red

Mountain that faces West Glenwood, is also made up of the ancient red sediment.

The volcanic vents that released the molten rock during the latest uplift never completely closed. The small fissures that remain continue to release not lava, but heated water. These hot springs spew forth water that has been enriched with minerals and heated deep with the earth's crust. It has been estimated that the water which bubbles to the surface today originally fell as rain some 20,000 years ago. The Siloam Springs, at the east end of Glenwood Canyon, and the larger, hotter Yampah Hot Springs at the western portal, have been pouring hot mineral water into the Colorado River for thousands of years.

*Descendents of some really early inhabitants of the valley (mule deer).*
(Courtesy of Frontier Historical Society - Shutte Collection)

There are a multitude of waterways that cascade down from the mountains of Western Colorado. One of the most energetic is the Roaring Fork River, which travels north from the ski mountains around Aspen. It absorbs the Frying Pan on the east and the Crystal on the west, and finally joins the larger Colorado River. The Colorado has its headwaters far to the northeast, and it joins the Eagle River just east of Glenwood Canyon. The combined waters of each of these drainages pound on westward, collecting other rivers and streams. Over the eons, they have patiently carved not only Glenwood Canyon, but also Glen Canyon in Southern Utah and the magnificent Grand Canyon. They fill Lake Powell, Lake Mead, and Lake Havasu, and eventually lose themselves in the deserts and irrigated fields of Arizona and California in the attempt to reach the Gulf of California.

The confluence of the Roaring Fork and the Colorado has, over the eons, formed a T-shaped valley. This wide expanse of reasonably flat land was punctuated, during the cold months, with plumes of steam from the many natural springs of hot mineral water. It was an inviting place, populated by herds of deer and elk, by magpies and by bald eagles. It remained this way for many thousands of years before it was ever seen by human eyes.

CHAPTER 2

# THE ORIGINAL INHABITANTS

No one knows when the Ute Indians first experienced the hot pools that line the banks of the Colorado River. It is not even a certainty that they were the first humans to frequent the area. It is known that they did come here on at least an annual basis for a great many centuries. They viewed the geothermal phenomenon as a sacred place, a gift from Manitou, their deity. They called the springs "Yampah", meaning "big medicine". Over the centuries, other tribes admired the relaxing, healing springs. Several battles were waged for their possession. However, the Utes were repeatedly successful in defending "their" hot springs.

*Trapper's Lake in the Flattops Wilderness Area - part of the ancestral hunting grounds of the White River Utes.* (Photo by the author)

The Utes were, and are, a unique tribe. When we think of powerful Indian tribes, we tend to envision the Comanche, the Apache, perhaps the Sioux. However, less than 10,000 Utes controlled most of Utah, almost all of Colorado, and parts of Wyoming and New Mexico for many hundreds of years. They were surrounded by others who coveted their land, Shoshones to the north, Cheyennes and Arapahos on the eastern Colorado plains, and Comanches and Apaches to the southeast.

The other tribes followed the herds of buffalo and other game, which occasionally led them into the huge area controlled by the Utes. When this occurred, they were met by tough, possessive warriors. The Utes were not especially aggressive, but they excelled at defending their land.

*Ute Indians in full regalia - about 1911.* (Courtesy of Frontier Historical Society)

Later, the Ute bands that occupied the southern portions of the territory were harried by the Spanish who controlled the Santa Fe area. To the consternation of the Spaniards, many of the meetings of the two peoples resulted in the Utes traveling back north with a collection of "borrowed" horses. It was about 1650 when the Utes and other tribes first acquired the horse from the Spaniards. The introduction of horses aided them tremendously in travel, in hunting, and in warfare. They became excellent riders, and before long the Spanish horses and their descendants became a large factor in the measure of individual wealth.

In addition to the warm waters at the edge of what was to become known as the Colorado River, the Utes discovered a series of caves that had been carved out of the limestone near the river. These caverns had been formed by millenniums of erosion. The Utes found the caves to be filled with warm vapors, sulfur-scented steam that eased their aches, relaxed and cleansed them.

Various small bands of Utes populated Western Colorado and most of Utah. They were primarily hunter-gatherers, moving in extended family groups to follow the seasonal abundance at various elevations. The men hunted deer, elk, antelope, and, rarely, buffalo with the bow and arrow and the spear. They also used arrows, snares, and nets to hunt rabbits, other small game and birds. The women gathered pinon nuts, roots, berries, seed grasses, and edible greens in woven baskets. Forked spears and elaborate fish traps were used to harvest the native trout that filled the rivers.

The Parianuc, or White River band of Utes, frequented the area that included the "Yampah" springs and vapor caves. As the white men encroached further and further into the Colorado mountains, the Utes felt increasing pressure from the outsiders. They signed a treaty in 1849, agreeing to remain at peace and to recognize the jurisdiction of the United States. In return, they were to retain possession of Western Colorado "forever". However, as has been

*Ute burial platform or hunting stand.* (Courtesy of Frontier Historical Society)

the case with so many tribes, that treaty and those that followed were routinely ignored by the white man.

The Ute Indians had spent untold centuries defending their land against other Indian tribes. They now found that the increasing numbers of whites also favored the grass-filled valleys, the game-filled hills. To make things even worse, news of gold and silver strikes were pulling droves of erstwhile miners into the mountains. Three prospectors named Bell, Blake, and Cleiopfar had followed an old Indian trail from the confluence of the Grand River (later the Colorado) and the Eagle River up onto the mountain range known as the Flattops. There they discovered rock formations similar to those at Leadville, Colorado, the site of a fabulous silver strike. The prospectors of course filed mining claims, the first of many to be filed around the carbonate formation, a layer of hardened sediment from an ancient lake bed. They were the first of 5,000 or so souls that came to Carbonate to seek their fortunes. Earlier, they had built a log fort in Wagon Gulch, another site of mining claims. The fort was close to the Canyon of the Grand and some distance southeast of the town site. They called it Fort Defiance. The name probably stemmed from their intention to occupy the area, treaty or no treaty.

Finally, in 1879, a relatively small number of warriors unintentionally brought the independence of the entire Ute tribe to an end. An Indian agent named Nathan Meeker was in charge of the White River Utes. He and many of the Indians lived next to the South Fork of the White River some fifty miles northwest of the Yampah springs. Meeker felt that the Utes should be forced to become farmers, that they should give up their heritage of hunting and living off the bounty provided by nature. Emotions became more and more heated, and finally the normally patient Utes exploded into violence. A war party led by a White River Ute Chief named Douglas attacked the settlement, killing Meeker and several other whites.

According to one account, they left Meeker's body pinned to the ground with a stake driven through his mouth, "To silence his infernal lying!" Meeker had sent for help in the person of Major T. T. Thornburgh and his troops. The army,

*Sign pointing out field on which Nathan Meeker was killed.* (Photo by the author)

*Monument to Nathan Meeker, killed by Ute Indians September 29, 1879.* (Photo by the author)

in advancing toward the agency, crossed Milk Creek, the boundary of the reservation. The Utes took this action to be an act of war and attacked them, killing Major Thornburgh and several of his men. This war party was led by another Ute chief named Colorow. The battles became known as the Meeker Massacre, and provided the excuse to remove both the White River band and the Tabeguache band to a reservation in Utah.

Thus ended an occupation of many centuries. The Utes had resisted the intrusion of other peoples since long before recorded history. However, they could not forever resist the relentless advance of progress, in the form of the white man. The Utes were forced away from their hot springs, their vapor caves, their sacred lands, their "Big Medicine".

There is little remaining evidence of the occupation of the Utes in and around Glenwood Springs. However, Indians from the three remaining Ute reservations met in Glenwood Springs in May of 1993, in a historic powwow. The celebration, which was the first meeting of its kind in

*Remains of Ute Wikiup - temporary shelter.* (Courtesy of Frontier Historical Society)

over 130 years, was repeated the following year. As part of the ceremonial activities, the Ute leaders and Forest Service personnel identified numerous sacred sites, locations of religious ceremonies such as "vision quests" in the surrounding forests.

Also, the Forest Service, working with the Utes and volunteers, has mapped an ancient path across the Flattops, the mountain range to the north of Glenwood. The trail was used by the Indians to access the game animals of the mountains, to visit the quarries for rocks suitable for the fashioning of tools and weapons. This path, part of which was later widened as a wagon road to Carbonate, begins at the east end of Glenwood Canyon near Dotsero and leads roughly northwest to the area of the South Fork of the White

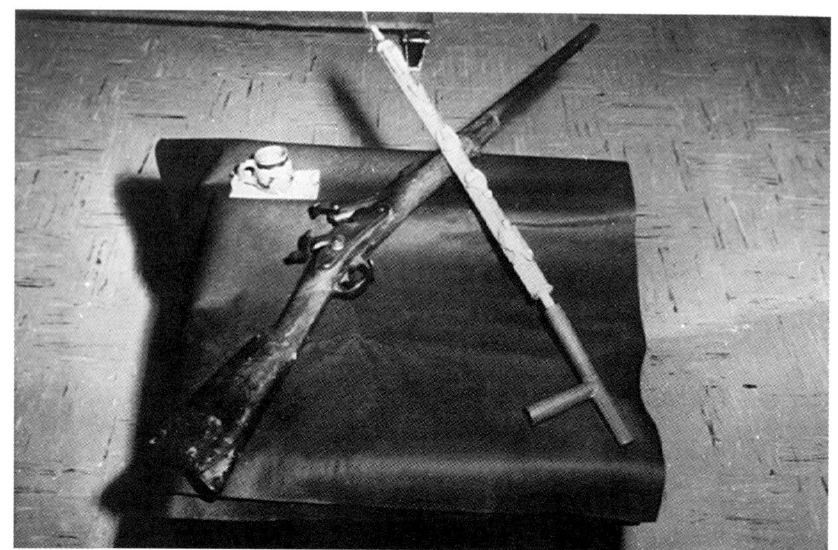

*Peace pipe and flintlock rifle which belonged to Colorow, now on display at the Meeker Museum, Meeker, Colorado.* (Courtesy of White River Museum)

*The Ute Trail, leading from the Dotsero area across the Flattops to the south fork of the White River.* (Courtesy of the US Forest Service)

River, where Meeker's agency was located. It meanders across the high, wild reaches, approaching 11,000 feet in elevation in places. It is known as the Ute Trail. The trail is dedicated to Frank "Slats" Olson, who was instrumental in its recognition.

If you walk the Ute Trail, or soak in the Hot Springs Pool, or relax deep in the vapor caves at the Yampah Spa, take a few quiet moments to see if you can feel the presence of the old ones, the Utes.

CHAPTER 3

# THE FIRST WHITE MEN

By the year 1500, America had been discovered. In 1607, Jamestown, the first English settlement in the new world, was established. The arrival of the Mayflower in 1620 marked the beginning of a seemingly endless stream of immigrants. The newcomers immediately began spreading westward in search of freedom, land, wealth, or simply adventure.

Why then did it take until 1860, almost 400 years, for the "white man" to discover the area that was to become Glenwood Springs? After all, by 1860, the first refrigerator had been invented, the first undersea communication cable had been laid, and more than 30,000 miles of railroad track had been laid in the eastern United States.

It helps to understand that, until the opening of Glenwood Canyon to rail and eventually to highway traffic, the valley of the hot springs was sort of tucked away, out of the traffic pattern. Oh, to be sure, there was traffic. As early as 1776, the Spanish Friars Dominguez and Escalante passed some fifty miles to the west on their quest for a route to California. They continued on, unaware of the existence of the valley of the "big medicine". In 1845, Captain John Fremont crossed the Flattops about twenty five miles to the north. Again, he had no clue of the existence of the pleasant valley.

In the 1800's, there were very probably mountain men in the area, solitary trappers and adventurers who lived like their only neighbors, the Indians. Quite possibly, a few of these visited the area of the Yampah Springs, but there is simply no written account of it.

In 1860, Richard Sopris, an explorer and prospector, crossed Cottonwood Pass from the Eagle River area to the location of present Carbondale, at the foot of the mountain which was to bear his name. He fell ill, and the local Utes advised his party to take him to the healing Yampah Springs. They brought him down the Thunder River, which we now call the Roaring Fork, to visit the miracle Indian springs. They built a raft to cross the Colorado River, then known as the Grand, and camped on an island at the site of the future Hot Springs Lodge. Sopris named the area Grand Springs. He was the first recorded non-Indian to use the healing waters.

Even after this discovery, it was almost 20 years later, in 1878, that James M. Landis made his way down the Roaring Fork Valley with a pack train. His aim was to harvest meadow hay for transportation back to Leadville. Leadville, which sits at roughly 10,000 feet, was by that time the home of some 40,000 gold and silver miners.

Landis basically fell in love with the valley. It was peaceful and inviting, especially compared to the bustle and the cold alpine winds of Leadville. The Utes welcomed him, and invited him to use the hogan that they had built at one of their springs. He returned the following spring, to file a

*Early settlers in the Yampah Springs valley.* (Courtesy of Frontier Historical Society)

squatter's right to 160 acres on the bank of the Roaring Fork. Under the watchful eyes of the resident Utes, he built a small log cabin. The following year, after the Meeker Massacre, the Indians in the valley were forced to relocate to the reservation in Utah. Landis was alone in his paradise until 1881, when his mother became the first white woman to enter the valley.

Isaac Cooper, a semi-invalid Civil War veteran, came to the area at about the same time. He had traveled to Aspen, which was on the verge of becoming a mining boom town. The supposedly curative powers of the hot springs drew him down valley. What he found filled him not only

*A drawing of Glenwood Springs as it appeared in 1883. The bridge shown had just been completed, but washed out the following spring. Note the island which became the location of the Hot Springs Lodge and Pool after Walter Devereux diverted the river so that it flowed to the right of the island.* (Courtesy of Frontier Historical Society)

with comfort and a sense of well-being, but also with a grand idea. He envisioned a great resort, a healing spa that would bring visitors from afar. With that in mind, he purchased the homestead from Landis for the princely sum of $1,500. The purchase price included the Yampah Springs. However, his paradise attracted few guests during the period of his ownership.

Even though the Utes were allowed to return to the valley each summer for the next few years, it was becoming clear that the influx of white settlers was to change the valley forever. In 1883, the Defiance Town and Land Company was formed, the name borrowed from the log fort up in Wagon Gulch. The new little town of Defiance grew slowly, tents and log cabins taking the place of the teepees of the Utes. In 1885, Sarah Cooper, the wife of Isaac, decided that "Defiance" just didn't convey the image of the kind of town in which she wanted to live. She and her husband Isaac had originally come from Glenwood, Iowa. History does not tell us what the city fathers thought of the idea, but Defiance shortly thereafter became Glenwood Springs.

CHAPTER 4

# DOC

In May of 1887, one of Glenwood Springs' most infamous citizens appeared on the scene. There are conflicting stories about the reason for his arrival, just as there are conflicting stories surrounding his "departure" in November of that year. Whatever the truth, John Henry "Doc" Holliday was to leave an abundance of legends in his wake.

Doc Holliday grew up in Griffin, Georgia as the Civil War was winding down. He was by all accounts a true southern gentleman, well dressed and soft spoken. As he matured, he developed two things which were to shape his later

*John Henry "Doc" Holliday - dentist, gambler, gunfighter.* (Courtesy of Frontier Historical Society)

life. First, though he was slender of build, his hands were unusually deft and strong. Those hands served him well in his first chosen profession as a dentist, and again a few years later as a gunfighter and gambler/cardsharp.

Second, like many of the population of his day, he contracted "consumption". We know it today as tuberculosis.

His tombstone, along with most publications, states incorrectly that he attended Dental School in Baltimore. The Catalogue of Graduates of the Pennsylvania College of Dental Surgery in Philadelphia lists a John H. Holliday as an 1872 graduate. Karen Holliday Tanner, descendent of the Holliday family and Doc Holliday historian, confirms that he did in fact graduate in Philadelphia. He set up an office in Atlanta for a short period of time. However, the heat and humidity of his native state served to aggravate his weakened lungs. Doctor John S. Holliday, Doc's uncle, originally diagnosed his tuberculosis. He recommended that Doc seek a drier climate. Doc headed west, and spent time wandering through Texas, Arizona, Kansas, South Dakota, and Colorado. He performed a little dentistry, became adept at dealing poker and faro, and developed a taste for whiskey.

It has been said that he also enriched several morticians in his travels. Estimates of the number of his victims range up to 25 or so. However, only one death has been conclusively proven, and the true number is probably much lower.

It is probably presumptuous to psychoanalyze someone who has been dead for over a hundred years, but a few things about the good doctor seem obvious. In the period of the late 1800's, law and order were sparse at best. The west of those days was filled with men who took what they wanted from the land and from each other, at the point of a gun if necessary. The saloons and gambling houses which Doc frequented were filled with these opportunistic, immoral folks. In order to exist in such an environment, a semi-invalid such as our friend Doc would have been forced to develop some impressive survival skills. In his case, those attributes apparently included an ability and a willingness to produce a variety of firearms when the need arose. He was known to carry a traditional six-shooter or two, as well as a derringer, or "hideout" gun. The derringer or his hunting knife could appear from his sleeve or his boot on a moment's notice. On at least one occasion, he was known to have worn a double-barreled 12 gauge shotgun, known as a "street howitzer", or an "alley cleaner" in those days, under his greatcoat. That occasion was the famous confrontation between Doc and the Earp brothers on the one side, and the Clantons and McLaurys on the other at the OK Corral in Tombstone, Arizona.

His acknowledged skill with his various weapons, coupled with the fact that tuberculosis was in many cases a death sentence, made him an extremely dangerous man. Perhaps in reaction to the hand dealt him by fate, he developed a violent temper. While he was still the southern gentleman when the mood struck him, he was at other times nothing more than a vicious, well-armed drunk with little fear of death. In the words of Wyatt Earp, "Although he sometimes drank three quarts of whiskey a day, he was still the most skillful gambler, and the nerviest, fastest, deadliest man with a six-gun I ever saw."

We know that Doc came to Glenwood Springs in May of 1887. Some say that he sought the healing hot springs and vapor caves of the Utes to relieve his consumption. Another story has it that he and Wyatt, a longtime friend, followed two men who had "offended" them down the Roaring Fork Valley, through Glenwood, and up onto the Flattops north of town. There, according to this version, Doc and Wyatt "put their lights out", and left them by a lake in the mountains. Upon returning to Glenwood Springs, Doc became too sick to travel. He remained in the little town while Wyatt headed back south.

Whatever the truth, Doc did remain in Glenwood. He lived in the newly built Hotel Glenwood that occupied the

*Photo frequently published as Doc Holliday - actually John Escapule of Bisbee, Arizona.* (Courtesy of John Tindall)

north-east corner of Eighth and Grand. The Hotel Glenwood burned in 1945, to be replaced by the building that now supports the clock tower. He again practiced a bit of dentistry. This fact perhaps speaks to the need for a dentist in Glenwood at that time, given that Doc was by then in the terminal stages of tuberculosis.

While legend has it that he left a trail of victims across the frontier west, he fought no gun battles in Glenwood. He dealt poker and faro in several of the saloons that had sprung up along the streets of Glenwood, and gradually grew weaker. In September, he lapsed into a coma which lasted almost two months. However, on the morning of November 8, he awoke and ordered a tumbler of whiskey. According to witnesses, he drank it with obvious satisfaction, said "This

*Memorial to Doc Holliday in the Linwood Cemetery, on a hill overlooking Glenwood Springs.* (Courtesy of John Tindall)

is funny!", in an apparent reference to the fact that he was dying with his boots off, and quietly did just that. He was 36 years old.

Just as there are several theories as to his reason for being in Glenwood, there are also numerous ideas as to his final resting place. Some say that he is buried somewhere in Linwood Cemetery, atop the hill to the east of town, and the monument erected in 1955 attests to that "fact". Again, another story has it that Doc and another unfortunate died at about the same time, and, given that the road to the cemetery was impassable due to mud and/or snow, that the both of them were interred at the base of the hill. The next spring, the family of the other man paid to have him exhumed and re-buried up the hill, while funds were not forthcoming to do a like favor for the Doctor. Consequently, according to that theory, he still rests somewhere in the east part of town, probably under someone's back yard.

Several years ago, some of Doc Holliday's relatives from Georgia came to Glenwood, demanding that he be dug up and delivered to them. The mayor at that time told the good folks from the South that if they could find him, they could have him. They obviously left town empty-handed.

An impressive monument has been erected to Doc Holliday in the Linwood Cemetery. It displays crossed six-guns and a poker hand. It is not uncommon to find flowers, playing cards, and occasionally, a shot of whisky left on the base of the tombstone.

Each August, during a weekend known as "Doc Hollidays", a group of locals reenact the Gunfight at the OK Corral. Doc is of course there, portrayed by a look-alike, along with the Earp brothers. The bad guys, the Clantons and the McLaurys, are also represented, along with a supporting cast. Hopefully, Doc would approve.

CHAPTER 5

# THE BIG POOL

Isaac Cooper had big plans for his spa at the location of the Yampah Springs of the Utes. However, as is usually the case, it took money to accomplish the feat. Money, in this case, came in the person of Walter Devereux.

Aspen had, by the 1880s, become the site of numerous high-grade silver mines. Devereux, a graduate of both Princeton and Columbia Universities, was brought to Aspen by Jerome Wheeler, owner of the Aspen Mine. Devereux was to manage the mine and construct a smelter for the processing of the ore. Finding the wood-fired smelters to be wanting, he investigated the lower reaches of the Roaring Fork Valley in search of coal. He found a thick seam of it in the mountains to the west of the Roaring Fork River, running from near the present site of Redstone past the New Castle area and on into northwestern Colorado.

*The Devereux brothers: from the left, Paul, Horace, James, Walter, and Alvin. Photo probably taken in New York about 1890.* (Courtesy of Frontier Historical Society)

Devereux proceeded to file claims to much of the coal reserves, either controlling them directly or leasing them to nearby settlements. He was a principal in the formation of the Grand River Coal and Coke Company, and shortly became a very wealthy man in his own right.

When Walter Devereux originally explored the area at the confluence of the Roaring Fork and the Colorado Rivers, he was approached by Isaac Cooper, who tried to interest him in the vision of a world-class spa. At that time, Devereux was much too busy getting rich, but his attitude was to change. Devereux had brought two of his brothers, Horace and James, to Aspen to share in the bonanza. The three of them, along with a group of British investors, eventually purchased the Yampah Springs and 10 acres of adjacent land from Cooper for $125,000.

Flush with his wealth from silver and coal mining and with the financial backing of a Lord Rathbone and other English investors, Devereux set out to build a complex that put even Isaac Cooper's dreams in the shade. His first goal was to build the world's largest hot springs pool. The Yampah Spring, the largest of the several springs in the immediate area and the one that was chosen to fill the envisioned pool, flows at 3,500,000 gallons a day. It comes out of the ground at 122 degrees Fahrenheit, or 51 degrees Celsius. Too hot for comfortable bathing, but the proximity of the snow-melt waters of the Colorado River provided a handy medium for tempering the hot mineral waters.

The big spring issued from the north bank of the Colorado. To develop the spa, it was first necessary build a rock wall to divert the flow of the Colorado to the south side of the island that sat in the middle of the river. This rather labor-intensive project was accomplished in part through the use of the local jail inmates. The influx of wealth to the area naturally brought with it those who would attempt to obtain a portion of that wealth through less than legal means. Many of the patrons of the saloons and gambling houses on Riverfront Street wound up working on the massive rock wall.

*Very early states of the construction of the Hot Springs Pool - 1896.*
(Courtesy of Frontier Historical Society)

The original pool, which was known as the Natatorium, was some 615 feet long, roughly two city blocks, and 75 feet wide. It ranged from 3 1/2 feet to 5 1/2 feet in depth, and sported a large fountain at the west end. It was completed in 1888.

For their next project, the Devereux brothers hired an architect from Vienna, Austria named Theodore von Rosenberg. His task was to design and construct a lodge and bathhouse to accompany their Natatorium. It was constructed of red "Peachblow" sandstone from a quarry up the Frying Pan Valley. The structure cost $100,000, and was completed in 1890. The building still stands next to the Hot Springs Pool, appearing much as it did upon its completion. The original interior was designed to rival the most luxurious spas of the world. It included English porcelain tubs and enamel walls in the Roman baths on the lower level. The second floor sported an exclusive, formal, men-only gambling casino, so that the privileged class could engage in their "gaming" without the necessity of rubbing elbows with the unwashed masses from the public gambling dens of Riverfront, now known as 7th Street. The spa also featured a lady's billiard room.

*During construction of the Hot Springs Pool - about 1887.* (Courtesy of Frontier Historical Society)

*The Hot Springs Pool after construction of the bathhouse.* (Courtesy of Frontier Historical Society)

*The Yampah mineral water - said to cure any number of ailments.* (Courtesy of Frontier Historical Society)

*The Hot Springs fountain in winter.* (Courtesy of Buzz Zancanella)

*The "Cocktail Spring." The young man in the center seems uncertain as to the taste.* (Courtesy of Frontier Historical Society)

*The Inhalatorium - exterior and interior - used for inhalation of the vapors from the hot mineral waters.* (Courtesy of Frontier Historical Society)

*Three brave souls enjoying the Hot Springs Pool in the dead of winter.* (Courtesy of Frontier Historical Society)

As part of the health complex, a small building known as the Inhalatorium was added, for the purpose of breathing the sulfurous vapors of the hot springs. Also, a "cocktail spring" provided goblets of the mineral-laden water for consumption by the guests. The

Yampah water was touted as a cure for just about anything, including rheumatism, obesity, gout, nervous strain, and male pattern baldness. Under the resident physician, a Dr. Schmitz, the water was bottled for some years and shipped worldwide. Travelers disembarking from the train were offered the chance to purchase bottles of the elixir. Records of miraculous cures are sparse, but then, there seems to be little indication that the administration of the magical waters ever killed anyone, either. The jury is, apparently, still out.

When President Taft visited Glenwood Springs in 1909, he declined an invitation to bathe in the big pool, saying that he "Was not built for public exhibition in a bathing suit."

Because of the temperature of the water, 90 degrees Fahrenheit or 32 degrees Celsius in the large pool and 104 degrees Fahrenheit or 40 degrees Celsius in the smaller, "hot" pool, it can be used year-round. Sitting in the healing waters surrounded by billowing clouds of steam is, and has always been, a magical experience, whether recovering from a hard day of working in a coal mine or of playing on a ski slope.

*Bathing "costumes" of the early 1900s.* (Courtesy of Frontier Historical Society - Schutte Collection)

CHAPTER 6

# THE ARRIVAL OF THE RAILROADS

By 1887, the year of Doc Holliday's death, the little town of Glenwood Springs was on the verge of a boom period that was to shape much of its future. Thanks to the investment of the Devereux brothers and their English backers, the financing was available for several giant strides in making Glenwood Springs available to the world.

It must be remembered that, up until the arrival of the white man in the valley and for some years thereafter, access to the Yampah Springs area was difficult, at best. Three routes existed. One led over Independence Pass, through Aspen, then down the Roaring Fork Valley from the south . Another, and in fact the route of the first stage line to run to the area, was over Cottonwood Pass to the south of "The Canyon of the Grand". (The Grand River did not officially become the Colorado until 1923.) The third approach was down Transfer Trail, a road which wound down the side of the mountain to the north. The rocky trail is still used as a 4 wheel drive road. It skirts Windy Point, a heart-stopping drop-off of several thousand feet which overlooks No Name Creek. The trail had been built to provide access to Carbonate, the town which had sprung up on the Flattops in response to an anticipated silver strike. Carbonate was the county seat of Garfield County for a short period of time, until an unusually harsh winter in 1883-1884 drove the settlers to move the county records down to Defiance, later Glenwood Springs. Carbonate was eventually abandoned, and little trace of the town is left.

Just west of Glenwood Springs, the Grand River valley narrowed to walls of almost vertical sandstone, closing off access to the open valleys beyond. This all but impassable cut was known as "Hell's Gate". Early travelers from the west went up Divide Creek, across "Haystack Gate", and down Four Mile Creek to Glenwood. On the east, the

*Sign at the site of Carbonate. The town of nearly 5,000 population was pretty much abandoned after the winter of 1893-1894 drove the residents down to the "Yampah Springs."* (Courtesy of Frontier Historical Society)

Grand River Canyon was a 16 mile stretch of deep, rugged, narrow gorge, so inaccessible that even the Indians had traditionally skirted it to the south over the Cottonwood Pass area or to the north via the Flattops and the Ute Trail.

Hell's Gate was finally widened in 1886 by J. D. Taylor. At about the same time, construction was progressing on the digging of tunnels and the blasting of ancient rock in the Grand River Canyon, preparatory to the laying of the first railroad tracks. Two railroad companies vied to be the first to reach Glenwood Springs; the Colorado Midland and the Denver and Rio Grande Western were embroiled in a race. For the victor awaited the lucrative coal carrying contracts from the mines which by then dotted the hills to the south and west of Glenwood.

The pending arrival of trains generated a high degree of excitement in the little town. The Devereux brothers were on the verge of realizing the anticipated throngs of affluent visitors to their spa. The coal mine owners and the ranchers and farmers were to be afforded easy transport of their

*Blasting during road construction in Glenwood Canyon.* (Courtesy of Frontier Historical Society)

products. Two banks opened, the First National and the Glenwood National. Hide Hall, a large two-story building, was constructed on the west side of Cooper Avenue to house the Glenwood Opera Company. The hall was used for opera, prize fights, town meetings, balls, and services by the Catholics, Methodists, Presbyterians, and Episcopalians. The madams of the Riverfront and Palmer Avenue red light district increased their "work force" to fifty, then to one hundred, and refurbished their places of business.

After two years of work in the canyon and over $2,000,000 in investment, construction was finally completed on the final obstacle, the 700 foot Jackson Tunnel just to the east of Glenwood. The Denver and Rio Grande Western Railroad entered Glenwood Springs from the east at about 7:45 P.M. on October 5, 1887. The first train, the 20 car "Little Giant", pulled through the Jackson Tunnel and into town to the accompaniment of fireworks, bonfires, candles, gunshots, and explosions of "giant powder" which had been used for the blasting in the canyon. Dignitaries from both the railroad and the town were on hand, and the celebrations were said to go on very late into the night.

Isaac Cooper, now 48 years of age but in ill health, was of course one of the distinguished citizens present at the ceremony. As "founder, pioneer, and benefactor" of Glenwood Springs, he was accorded the honor of riding the train into town, to be greeted by music, a cacophony of sound, and the cheers of some 3,500 of his fellow citizens. Unfortunately, he was in the final stages of his illness, and he almost immediately took to his bed. He remained there until his death on December 2. Perhaps fittingly, after lying in state in the lobby of the Hotel Glenwood, his body was transported by train to Denver, where he was buried in Riverside Cemetery.

The D&RGW arrived in Glenwood Springs 68 days ahead of the Midland Railroad, which was being built down the Roaring Fork Valley from Basalt. The celebration for the arrival of the Midland was muted in comparison to that for the D&RGW, partially because of the death of Isaac Cooper.

With the arrival of the railroads, the little valley was finally open to easy access by the world. It only remained for Edward Taylor, District Attorney of the 9th Judicial District, to propose and promote the construction of what was to become known as the "Taylor State Road", the first wagon road from Denver through the Grand River Canyon to Grand Junction. He was elected to the state senate on the issue, and in 1899 sponsored a bill to allocate $40,000 in state aid for the project. The road took three years to complete, and wound up costing $60,000, half of which was expended in the Grand River Canyon. Interestingly, especially for the turn of the century, it was specified that trees and other plant life were to be preserved whenever possible, and roadside advertising was prohibited. The first road through the canyon was crude, to be sure, but the first of many millions of automobiles was to traverse it in 1902. Automotive tourism to the Glenwood Springs area was born with a whimper that held no clue as to the giant that it was to become.

*The Taylor State Road through Glenwood Canyon - the first wagon raod from Denver to Grand Junction.* (Courtesy of Frontier Historical Society - Shutte Collection)

CHAPTER 7

# BLACK GOLD

The coal deposits discovered by Walter Devereux were of the soft, or bituminous variety. Compared to the harder and scarcer anthracite coal, bituminous was considered to be the more valuable. Not only could it be used for home heating in its original form, but it might also be heated under low oxygen conditions to produce other products. Bituminous coal tends to melt under such conditions, releasing coal tars and gases. The coal tars were later used in the manufacture of such things as aspirin, explosives, and embalming fluid. The gases may be used as fuel, or in dyes and insecticides.

However, the most valuable product of the heating process is known as "coke". It is a hard, grayish-black fuel that produces intense heat with no smoke. It is used extensively in the smelting of metals. It was just such coal that Mr. Devereux was seeking for his employer's silver mines in Aspen.

*The town of Cardiff, about 1900.* (Courtesy of Frontier Historical Society)

*Remains of Cardiff coke ovens, used to change coal into "coke," to be used in the smelting of metal ore.* (Photo by the author)

In the late 1800s, the coking process was performed in "coke ovens," beehive-shaped structures of firebrick with vents at the top and in one side of the base. Lines of these ovens may still be seen outside Redstone and along the old Cardiff road south of Glenwood Springs. The facing stones which are visible in the old photos have long since become paving stones and fireplaces for local homes, as well as part of a retaining wall for the Hot Springs Pool, but some of the conical ovens themselves remain. Cardiff became the major coking center for the area, with some 240 ovens in all. Many of them have fallen into disrepair or disappeared completely. However, the remaining ovens still show the yellow firebrick, the inside surfaces melted and fused to almost a glass-like consistency by the incredible heat of the coking process. It is said that the glow of the fires in the ovens could be seen reflecting from the bottoms of the clouds from as far away as New Castle, some 12 miles distant. The coke ovens wasted the tars and the gases, but that was not a concern at that time. Devereux had found what he needed, and the coal mining industry was born in the Glenwood Springs area. Later, pipes were laid to the ovens to capture the coal gas, which was used in heating.

In the following years, numerous coal mines were dug along "Coal Ridge", the thick black seam that ran from above Redstone to the New Castle area. The town of Sunshine, later changed to Sunlight, sprung up along Four-Mile Creek, not far below the present site of the Sunlight Ski Area. Only the bleached bones of a few buildings remain to mark its location. Other mines and the accompanying towns were formed at Coal Basin, Spring Gulch, Marion, South Canyon, and New Castle.

Many of the small coal mining towns of that period were company towns. They were set up to provide housing, schools, and other necessities for the miners. However, for many of the miners, these towns were a trap. Most of the men who spent 12 hours a day underground were immi-

*The mining town of Sunlight in 1910.* (Courtesy of Buzz Zancanella)

*Loads of coal brought out of South Canyon on sleds.* (Courtesy of Frontier Historical Society)

grants from Italy or Greece, from Austria or Mexico. The immigrants were tied to the mine owners by contract. They had contracted with agents who paid their transportation costs and guaranteed to the United States Immigration Authorities that they would be gainfully employed. In return, the agents received an assignment of the miner's wages until the transportation costs plus a large profit were paid. It was a form of indentured servitude.

Because their families were not immediately able to join them, it was a lonely existence for many of the miners. Consequently, it was doubly vital that they work to the satisfaction of the owners. In those days, there was no unemployment insurance, no paid vacation, sick leave, or medical benefits. If a worker was unable to produce, he would simply be replaced. Mining being what it is, there were instances of men leaving their family and their native land and subsequently dying in a cave-in or an explosion. The families of these unfortunates might never find out the fate of their loved one.

Once the miner was able to bring his wife and family to America, his troubles did not cease. For his needs and those

*Coal miner with his children and his assistant.* (Courtesy of Frontier Historical Society)

of his family, he received script that could only be redeemed at the company store. Many times, it was the efforts of the wife and children that were the deliverance for the family. Land was still available for homesteading, and many of the homesteads in the mountains around Glenwood Springs were claimed in the name of the wives of the miners. The sale of farm products, fresh baked bread, or laundry and cleaning services brought many of the families closer to the level of prosperity of the rest of the area.

In later years, as the local mines closed, the Greeks tended to move on to work the coal mines in Cameo or in Palisade. Many of the Italians, Austrians, and Mexicans stayed in the area, becoming farmers, ranchers, or businessmen.

Coal mining is, and has always been, a dangerous profession. The sometimes extreme angles of the Colorado coal seams produce difficult, hazardous working conditions. Heavy machinery, in and of itself, carries with it the threat of injury; the same may be said of the explosives used to loosen the coal. Water, in the form of underground springs or reservoirs was a constant problem. Coal dust, created by breaking up the coal for processing can cause black lung disease, with its accompanying shortness of breath and of life. The dust can also be explosive. Coal mines tend to produce noxious gases, most notably methane. The early miners referred to methane as "fire damp". The coal itself was formed when thick layers of rotted plant material from ancient swamps were covered and subjected to pressure and heat. When the heat is intense, such as that produced by the igneous rock that was forced upwards to form Mount Sopris, methane gas is formed within and around the coal. Methane is not only poisonous, but it is also highly volatile. Methane explosions touched off by sparks from machinery or simply from metal tools have caused the injury or death of many miners. Especially in the early days of coal mining, the use of torches and explosives caused a very realistic concern on the part of the miners.

Working deep within the earth carries with it the obvious possibilities of rockfalls or cave-ins, trapping or crushing the miners. Removing rock and coal from within the mountain can result in "bumps" or "bounces" when the earth rearranges itself to accommodate the voids. Depending on the severity of the movements, they can range from annoying to deadly.

In 1896, 47 men were killed in an explosion in the Vulcan Mine near New Castle. In 1913, the mine blew again, killing 37. That particular mine was quite gaseous, and was infamous for fires. It blew again in 1918, claiming 3 more victims. It was finally closed permanently, with a fire in progress. On the mountainside across the Colorado River from New Castle, there is a broad band where the vegetation is sparse, and where the snow never collects. Deep within the coal seam that runs beneath the surface, that fire still smolders.

On September 3, 1897, an explosion at the Sunshine Mine killed twelve men. There were said to be unusually strong air currents that day, which might have added oxygen to the resulting fire.

On September 16, 1901, The Spring Gulch Mine blew, killing six miners. The cause of the explosion was never determined with any certainty, but it was reported that a watch belonging to one of the doomed miners was blown out of one of the air shafts.

By the 1950s, most of the old mines had been abandoned. The major exception was the series of mines operated by Mid-Continent Resources some 10 miles west of Redstone. The Dutch Creek No. 1 mine was quite productive. It also held extensive pockets of methane. It has been estimated that the No. 1 mine released 1.5 million cubic feet of methane every 24 hours. The mine was classified as "potentially hazardous", due to the high concentrations of methane. Nine miners were killed in the shaft in a methane blast in 1965.

On April 15, 1981, 22 men were working in the Dutch Creek No. 1 mine. About 4:15 in the afternoon, there was a massive explosion some 7,200 feet from the surface. The blast knocked out both the ventilation system and the communications system, making rescue efforts even more hazardous. A short time after the explosion, three men emerged from the mine entrance uninjured. Then, a rescue team brought out four more men, all alive but with varying degrees of burns or other injuries.

As families of the 15 men still missing set up a vigil around campfires on the mountainside below the mine entrance, rescue teams inched their way along the 13 degree slope toward the area of the explosion. Finally, a day and an half after the blast ripped through the lower reaches of the mine, nine of the miners were found. It appeared that they had died instantly. As one miner put it, "Being near a methane explosion in a mine shaft would be like being in an exploding gun barrel." About three hours later another five were found, and the fifteenth and last body was discovered another three hours later. The vigil of the families was at last over.

The Mid-Continent mines were re-opened shortly after the disaster, but have since been closed permanently.

CHAPTER 8

# THE VAPOR CAVES

When Richard Sopris first laid eyes on the healing hot springs at the west end of the Grand River Canyon, they were pretty much as the Utes had found them some centuries before. The Indians constructed a hogan next to one of the springs, but that was about it. The existing limestone caves had also been in use by the Utes. They normally utilized them for the therapeutic effects of the hot vapors, but sometimes they were used as punishment for errant braves. While a short time in the heated steam was quite soothing and pleasant, apparently being barricaded underground with the temperature exceeding a hundred degrees proved to be disagreeable, bordering on terrifying.

In those days, there were many separate springs on both sides of the river and on an island in the middle. Estimates range from 13 to about 50. Most were small, but the main one, the one that was later to be used for the Hot Springs Pool, produced a quite impressive flow of 122 degree water. The earliest recorded commercial use of the steady flow of hot mineral water was by a Jonas Lindgren. Lindgren apparently suffered from rheumatism. The Indians had told him of the healing qualities of the springs, so in 1881 he, probably painfully, hewed enough wood to construct a bathtub. He would partially fill it with a bucket from the hot spring, then cool the scalding mineral water with water from the river. Having achieved a bearable temperature, he would immerse himself in the tub and soak.

According to Jonas, the waters did in fact relieve his aches and pains. Before long, stage and freight drivers were stopping by for a soak. They also soaked the hooves and ankles of their horses; it was reported the horses seemed to enjoy it. Jonas, apparently a man to take advantage of an opportunity, began charging ten cents for the use of the tub. The bathers had to carry their own water, and Jonas provided neither towel, roof, nor privacy, but no one seemed to mind all that much. The minerals in the water were said to cure influenza and the occasional case of lead poisoning, in addition to rheumatism.

The fame of the hot springs was spreading. Glenwood Springs, indeed the entire state of Colorado, was being touted as a haven of clean air and healing waters. If in fact Doc Holliday did come to Glenwood seeking a cure for his lung disorder, he was not alone. It was stated, with perhaps a bit of exaggeration, that it took twice as much killing to finish off a man in Colorado. Horse thieves reportedly required an additional five minutes of hanging to finish the job. No less a worthy than P.T. Barnum, who was admittedly given to a degree of exaggeration, is quoted as saying, "Two-thirds of them came here to die and they can't do it!" Another traveler stated that in some sections of Colorado it was so healthy that a man had to be killed to start a cemetery.

The original vapor caves, which eventually became known as the "Old Cave", or Cave No. 1, were located on the south bank of the Grand River. The Indians and a few of the early settlers took advantage of the natural Turkish baths. The main cave was used year round. An additional opening was constructed in the hillside so that the ailing and infirm could be lowered to the floor of the cave on a stretcher, there to hopefully sweat out their particular demons. After the Meeker Massacre and the resulting ouster of the Utes, the population of the valley and the usage of the cave by the whites both increased. For the sake of modesty, men used the cave in the mornings, and the ladies in the afternoon. The charge for the use of the cave was 25 cents. In 1883, the Defiance Town and Land Company set about to construct a new cave about 100 feet west of the original one. Not surprisingly, this was to become known as Cave No 2. There is some question whether this cave was ever actually excavated.

By 1887, the railroad was coming to Glenwood Springs, the Hot Springs Pool was under construction, and the Devereux brothers were intent on making their complex into

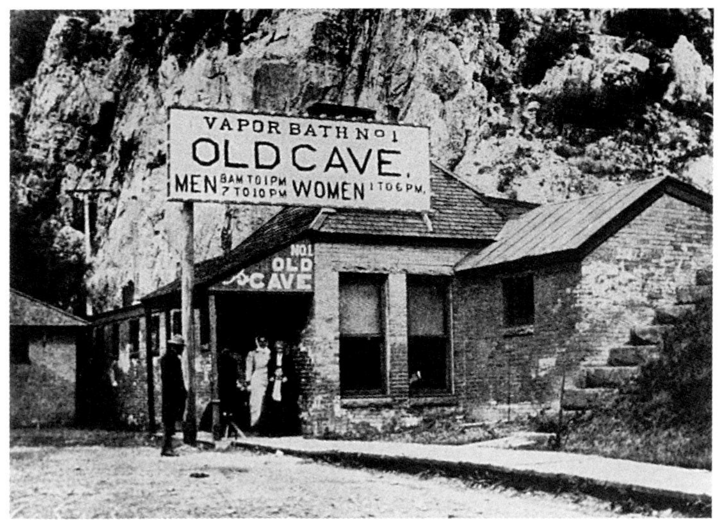


*Cave No. 1, on the south side of the Grand River (later Colorado). Site of the original Ute cave.* (Courtesy of Buzz Zancanella)

a world-class spa. Some $40,000 was spent in digging yet another tunnel, this time on the north side of the river. The impetus for the excavation was the spring from which the 122 degree water issued. This was the hottest of the springs.

This tunnel went into the solid limestone of the mountain some 35 feet, and three large caverns were excavated. With only a little diversion the water was made to flow through these rooms, creating yet another underground steam bath for the residents and the increasing flow of tourists. The new caves boasted an enclosed entrance, electric lights from the new hydroelectric plant next door, and marble benches. After the new cave, aptly named "Cave No. 3", went into operation, the construction of the railroad sealed off the original Ute caves. The patrons of the newest cave still observed separate bathing times for men and women. Also, they were apparently a bit more modest than were the customers of Jonas Lindgren. Both sexes wore heavy linen bags, open at both ends and with a drawstring at the neck. Not terribly fashionable, but no doubt proper. A large hourglass was provided so that the patrons could time their stay.

In 1893, construction was begun on the Vapor Caves build-

*Interior of "Cave No. 3" - the Vapor Caves.* (Courtesy of Frontier Historical Society)

*Interior of "Cave No. 3," showing marble benches.* (Courtesy of Frontier Historical Society)

ing which sits on the site today. Over the intervening years, the succeeding owners have enlarged and improved the property. They left the century-old caves much as they were, but have individual massage rooms, Jacuzzi baths, and a salon.

CHAPTER 9

# THE HOTEL COLORADO

When Walter Devereux was planning his spa complex, which of course included the great pool and the vapor caves, he wanted a hotel that would match his vision. He retained the architectural firm of Boring, Tilton, & Mellon from New York City. They designed a massive structure, modeled after the Villa de Medici, a 16th century Italian mansion. Like the Hot Springs Lodge, the Hotel Colorado was constructed partly of sandstone from Wilson's Peachblow Quarry up the Frying Pan River, and partly from Roman brick. The building is 260 feet deep, 224 feet wide, and surrounds on three sides an open courtyard some 124 feet on a side. To match the fountain in the pool, the Florentine fountain in the center of the courtyard sent a jet of water 185 feet into the air. The construction cost was $850,000, a staggering sum . Construction began in August of 1892, and the grand opening was June 10, 1893.

*Nineteen hundred-era postcard showing the height of the fountain in the courtyard of the Hotel Colorado.* (Courtesy of Scott Leslie)

*Exterior of the Hotel Colorado, showing the open south court.* (Courtesy of Frontier Historical Society)

The interior of the hotel matched the opulence of the exterior. The east and west wings were joined by an open lobby. The east wing housed the more expensive suites, a dining room, a play room and nursery, and the Lady's Billiard Room. In the west wing were a music room and a large ball room. Across the lobby from the open south court was another dining room. It boasted a ceiling to floor waterfall which fell into a crystal-clear pool. The pool was landscaped to resemble a mountain clearing, and was home to native trout. The full basement contained a men's bar and billiard room, a tunnel to the servant's quarters, baths, and a huge room under the dining room and kitchen which was capable of holding 300 tons of ice.

The upper floors contained 200 Victorian guest rooms, with some 40 private bathrooms. Two grand stairways curved up from the lobby level, and a hydraulic elevator, likely the first on the Western Slope of Colorado, carried guests between floors. The entire hotel, indeed, the entire town of Glenwood Springs was lit by electric lights, surely a

*Waterfall in the dining room of the Hotel Colorado. The pool was home to native trout. Early 1900s.* (Courtesy of Frontier Historical Society)

novelty to many of the early guests. Such personages as David Moffitt, the Mayo Brothers, the Goulds, the Astors, and Diamond Jim Brady visited the hotel during the opening festivities or in the following years. The Hotel Colorado had joined the Brown Palace in Denver as one of Colorado's premium hostelries. In the early years, the hotel was open only during the warm months, from about May to October, as it had no central heating.

The Hotel Colorado has hosted many notables in its 100 plus years of operation. President William Howard Taft made an address from the Presidential Balcony, as did Teddy Roosevelt. When Teddy came to Glenwood in April of 1905 for a bear hunt, the hotel became the Western White House for the duration of his visit. According to local legend, he returned from the hunt one day empty-handed. The hotel maids stitched together a small bear from scraps of cloth and presented it to the President to lift his spirits. Thus was born the Teddy Bear, named by a local reporter.

*Hotel Colorado bridal suite. Early 1900s.* (Courtesy of John Tindall)

The hotel has also been graced with the presence of Al Capone and fellow gangster Diamond Jack Alterie. Tom Mix stayed there during the filming of "The K & A Train Robbery", in 1926. In more recent years, Patrick Swayze slept at the hotel while Disney Studio's "Tall Tales" was being produced.

According to many of the hotel employees and several of the visitors over the years, there are certain non-paying guests that roam the halls of the Hotel Colorado. It is said that doors will occasionally open or close without the apparent aid of human hand. The elevator will supposedly move between floors of its own accord. The smell of cigar smoke in the lobby has been noted on several occasions, with no known source. Likewise, the perfume of a murdered chambermaid is sometimes detected in what is now known as the Devereux Room. Gentleman guests sleeping in the bell towers have been startled, to put it mildly, to awaken and find the figure of a woman standing over them. A mysterious form in gray slacks and a red and white vest appeared in the early 1980's, and again in 1993, and was said to have

*President Theodore "Teddy" Roosevelt during his 1905 hunting trip to Glenwood Springs.* (Courtesy of Frontier Historical Society)

then vanished. The figure of a young girl, complete with lacy Victorian dress, has been spotted playing with a ball on the grand staircase.

In 1943, in the midst of World War II, the Hotel Colorado was commissioned as a Navy hospital. By then, much of the plumbing and electrical wiring was in need of attention, and the Navy did a great deal of repairing and modernizing of the building. They also installed an automatic fire protection system. The Hot Springs Pool and the Vapor Caves were essentially closed to the public, and were reserved for the use of the recuperating military personnel. The hotel and the other facilities were returned to civilian use in early 1946.

*Tom Mix and "Tony" in Glenwood Canyon during the filming of* The K & A Train Robbery *in 1926.* (Courtesy of Frontier Historical Society)

Devereux did indeed create a world-class spa, with the big pool, the vapor caves, and the luxurious Hotel Colorado. Glenwood Springs has played host to the wealthy and the famous from all over the world. The D&RGW siding which had been constructed to deliver building materials to the Hotel Colorado was left as a siding for the private railroad cars which carried many of the prominent guests. However, the Silver panic of 1893, just two months after the opening of the hotel, signaled troubled times to come. When the Government demonetized silver, it literally turned the former boom towns of Leadville and Aspen into ghost towns almost overnight. Glenwood Springs was not directly effected by the panic, and newly rich Coloradans continued to rub shoulders with wealthy British tourists.

*The courtyard fountain in winter.* (Courtesy of Buzz Zancanella)

Unfortunately, the salad days of the magnificent hotel were not to last. In the intervening years the hotel has changed hands many times, mostly through sales, but also through foreclosure and even a tax sale. In 1961, part of the hotel was used as classrooms for the junior high students. In the early 1970s, the name was changed to "Village Inn" and major remodeling was undertaken, with the view of utilizing the building however possible. The new name did not stick, however, and the name "Hotel Colorado" returned.

The 1990s have seen more remodeling, the principal aim of which has been to recapture much of the elegance and charm which was experienced by the likes of Presidents Roosevelt and Taft. The walls of the lobby are lined with pictures which reflect the history of the grand old hotel.

CHAPTER 10

# ...AND OTHER BUILDINGS

The Hotel Colorado and the Hot Springs Lodge and Pool are the most prominent of the old structures in Glenwood Springs. However, there are many other buildings with as rich a history. Because of the nature of the times, several of the older buildings were either a saloon, a brothel, or both at one time or another. One of the early residents, John Blake, who had been instrumental in the construction of Fort Defiance, and who later served as Sheriff, had a common-law wife named Gussie. An enterprising woman, she became the first madam in the fledgling town of Defiance. Because of the lure of the hot springs, the saloons, and the "sporting houses", Defiance and later Glenwood Springs became a popular weekend destination for the miners and cowboys from the surrounding hills. Even when the fledgling city was nothing but a collection of tents, there were

*"Riverfront," now 7th Street, about 1883. A mixture of saloons, brothels, gambling halls, and other establishments.* (Courtesy of Frontier Historical Society)

*Fred Barlow and his dugout. One of the first structures in "Defiance," it served as a hotel, post office, and the Garfield County Court House. About 1883.*
(Courtesy of Frontier Historical Society)

saloons, and, presumably, Gussie Blake. Blake Avenue was named for one of the Blakes. History does not reveal which one was accorded the honor.

One of the earliest log structures in the new little town was a dugout owned by Fred Barlow. The crude building served, at various times, as Garfield County's first court house, as the post office, and as the Barlow Hotel. In fact, the town was listed in postal records as "Barlow" from June 1883 to March 1884.

Glenwood Springs was one of the first cities in the world with a hydroelectric plant. The completion of the plant in 1886 brought Glenwood from the era of kerosene and candles directly to the age of electricity, without the intervening use of gaslamps, as with many towns of the period. The electric plant building, at 601 6th Street, has since been converted to the Glenwood Springs Center for the Arts.

The first railroad station, which served the D&RGW line, was located at 7th and Pitkin. Another station, the sandstone building at 413 7th Street, was built in 1904. It

*The D&RGW railroad station between 7th Street and the Colorado River.*
(Courtesy of Frontier Historical Society)

now serves as Glenwood's only railroad station.

Across 7th Street from the railroad station is the Hotel Denver. It has been remodeled several times over the years. The block originally began as Bosco's Wholesale Liquor and Saloon, the Columbus Saloon, and Sheridan's Senate Bar. Furnished rooms in the buildings became the Denver Hotel and the Star Hotel. As the years went by, the various buildings were melded into the present hotel/office building operation. The most recent renovation added a restaurant/ brew pub.

In 1884, a small brick hotel was built at the corner of 8th and Grand Avenue. It was the original Hotel Glenwood. In the next two years, a wooden addition increased the building to a modern (for the date) three story hotel. The style was Victorian, and balconies were added. Prior to the opening of the Hotel Colorado, the Hotel Glenwood was the premier hotel in the area. H.A.W. Tabor, the Silver King, and his attractive young wife, Baby Doe, were frequent guests. Both Doc Holliday and Isaac Cooper died there. The hotel

*The south side of 7th Street, across from the D&RGW station. From the left, the Rex Hotel, the Star Hotel, and the Hotel Denver. The Star and the Denver have since combined into one building.* (Courtesy of Frontier Historical Society)

*The Leadville Bar, in the Hotel Denver, owned by Henry Bosco.* (Courtesy of Frontier Historical Society)

*The Hotel Glenwood, at the corner of 8th and Grand, about 1887.* (Courtesy of Frontier Historical Society)

burned in 1945, and was replaced with the building which was recently remodeled, and the clock tower added.

On the north side of the Hotel Glenwood, there was a narrow room which was originally used as a sample room for traveling salesmen. Later, it was converted to a barber shop by Billy Stiles, one of the early black residents. It remained a barber shop until 1997, when it became Narcissus, a beauty salon. The narrow building is the only remaining portion of the Hotel Glenwood.

The Silver Club Building, at 715 Grand Avenue, was built in 1895. The lower floor was a saloon, the large room in the front of the second floor was a private high stakes gambling hall, and the small rooms which made up the remainder of the second floor were utilized by "ladies of the evening". Later uses for the building included a welding shop. In 1976, the Defiance Community Theater Company remodeled the building into a dinner theater. Later, the building was again redone, this time into retail shops, offices, and an Italian restaurant.

*The Hotel Glenwood in 1945, just after it was consumed by fire. Six died in the blaze.* (Courtesy of Frontier Historical Society)

The Glenwood Shoe Repair and King's Barber Shop are housed in the oldest building in downtown Glenwood. It was built in 1884, and was originally the Mirror Saloon and Wholesale Liquors. The building still sits on the original cedar post foundation. The present day saloon that carries the Doc Holliday name has been a landmark and a collection of Holliday memorabilia since the 1960's. Prior to that, it was a jewelry store, a bar, and a restaurant.

The building that presently houses the Frontier Historical Society Museum at 1001 Colorado Avenue was built in 1905. The original owners were Dr. & Mrs. Marshall Dean. George Edinger, a private banker, later purchased the home and ultimately willed it to his daughter and her husband, Stella and Churchill Shumate. The Shumates in turn willed the house to the Historical Society. It has been used as a museum since 1971, and holds a wealth of artifacts and information about the Glenwood Springs area.

At 312 7th Street, the Fraternal Order of the Eagles #215 now occupies the building that was built in 1890 as

*Glenwood's first jail, a 12 x 12 foot cement structure, now sits in Veltus Park.* (Courtesy of Frontier Historical Society)

the Odeon Theater. It featured live theater, and the pulleys, scenery weights and catwalk, as well as some 1890's graffiti still exist. It was later converted to a silent movie house. Tom Mix performed there in 1926, while he was filming his movie in the canyon.

The first service at the First Presbyterian Church at 1016 Cooper Avenue was October 6, 1887. The pastor, a Reverend Rudolph, conducted funeral services for Doc Holliday later that year. President Benjamin Harrison worshipped at the church in 1891. Teddy Roosevelt attended services in 1905 during his famous hunt.

The Glenwood Sanitarium at 512 10th Street was completed in 1908. It was built under the guidance of Dr. W. F. Berry. He also started and ran a nurse's training school at that location. The operation and the school were both forced to close during the Depression. The old sanitarium has since been converted to apartments.

CHAPTER 11

# STRAWBERRY DAYS

By 1886, several large and productive farms and orchards had been established in the Roaring Fork, Eagle, and Grand River valleys. Among the more popular crops was the strawberry. The Tri-County Farmer's Union was formed to stimulate demand for farm products. It was felt that some sort of annual celebration would be an excellent method of promoting both the crops and the area. Over the next year or so, there was more and more talk amongst the group about the possibilities of a special day.

The farmer's group approached the leaders of Glenwood Springs in early 1898 with the idea, touting the benefits to the town. As excitement began to grow, there was talk of prizes for fruit and flower displays, of recreational possibilities, of visitors from afar. It wasn't long before the date of June 18, 1898 was set for the first Strawberry Day Festival.

*Grand Avenue on the very first Strawberry Day, June 18, 1898.* (Courtesy of Buzz Zancanella)

*Block-long tables were used to serve the free fresh strawberries and cream at the early Strawberry Days. This picture is from 1910.* (Courtesy of Frontier Historical Society - Schutte Collection)

The following four months saw increasing promotional efforts for the upcoming celebration. Everyone in Colorado who read a newspaper was invited. Governor Alva Adams received a special invitation. It was proposed that everyone in the area include an image of "a pretty, juicy looking strawberry" on their stationary. The D&RGW Railroad offered special round trip rates, and brought hundreds of passengers from both east and west. The Colorado Midland not only brought many celebrants into town, but also provided a 30 member uniformed band that set up at 8th and Grand and played a concert for the gathering masses. More visitors arrived by horseback and by carriage. All told, the first Strawberry Day drew 2,500 people to Glenwood Springs.

There was, as promised, music and floral displays and a baseball game against the team from Leadville. (Glenwood Springs won, 6-5.) There was free admission to the great pool, and an evening ball with the Colorado Midland band again providing the melodies.

*Strawberry Days parade entry. Coach may (or may not) have carried Doc Holliday.* (Courtesy of Frontier Historical Society)

*Tightrope walker over the Colorado River - part of the 1912 Strawberry Days celebration.* (Courtesy of Frontier Historical Society - Schutte Collection)

However, the activity which made the day special to all concerned, the crowning glory of the activities, was the serving of fresh-baked cake, covered with strawberries and drowned with fresh cream. Best of all, the delicious treat and the accompanying lemonade were free to all comers. Naturally, much of the work of baking the cakes and preparing the strawberries fell upon the ladies of Glenwood, but hopefully the pleasure of the huge crowd was adequate thanks. The ladies might have felt more gratified, had they known that their Strawberry Day was the first of a series of celebrations that would go on for over a century.

The annual celebration has changed over the intervening years. The addition of a parade offered local businesses and organizations the opportunity to advertise their products, entertain the crowd, or just celebrate their existence. There have been rodeos, auto races, boat races, bicycle races, and little yellow plastic duck races down the Roaring Fork River. Airplane barnstormers and a gentleman who walked a tightrope over the Colorado River have drawn gasps from the crowd. Humbert Reese, a long-time columnist for the *Glenwood Post*, recalls watching a human fly climb the northeast corner of the Citizen's building without benefit of ladder, rope, or net. Another daredevil in another year dove from the Grand Avenue bridge into the Colorado River. There have been prize fights, polo matches (in the early years), swimming/diving meets, and tennis and golf tournaments. Volleyball tourneys, softball games, and mountain bike races have drawn contestants from the entire state.

The Strawberry Shortcut was instituted in 1978. It features both a 5K and a 10 K run/walk. It has grown from 232 entrants the first year to an average of over 1,200 per year. It is a competitive run for some, a social event for others.

A carnival, in the form of a single merry-go-round and a few concessions, was added early on. Like most of the activities, it has grown over the years.

In 1913, another enduring tradition was begun. Miss Ruby Clark became the first of a long list of beautiful and talented Strawberry Days Queens. Like many similar activities, this one began as a beauty contest. There was the obligatory evening gown and talent events, and in some

*Ada Hutchings, the Strawberry Days Queen of 1915.* (Courtesy of Frontier Historical Society)

years, a swim suit competition. In order to court political correctness, the title was changed in 1991 from Strawberry Days Queen to Strawberry Days Ambassador. This change was met with something less than enthusiasm, so 1992 brought about "Miss Strawberry Days Ambassador". That unwieldy moniker was shortened to Miss Strawberry Days, and so it remains. Also, the competition has been changed to a scholarship contest. In 1997, the winner received a $1,500 scholarship. The First runner-up received $1,000, and third place received $500. The contestants are judged on communication skills, self esteem, poise, and knowledge of the community. Whatever the criteria, each year's Miss Strawberry Days is indeed an ambassador for the city of Glenwood Springs.

*Strawberry Day - about 1905. The display contained live deer and bighorn sheep.* (Courtesy of Frontier Historical Society)

Strawberry Days has grown a great deal in the last century; activities cover most of a week now. The celebration now attracts guests from all over the country. However, one thing has not changed. Although strawberries are no longer grown commercially anywhere in the valley, that has not prevented the city of Glenwood Springs from serving free strawberries and ice cream to many thousands of visitors each year.

In 1997, the 100th anniversary of that first Strawberry Day, the celebration drew some 30,000 people to Glenwood Springs.

CHAPTER 12

# RECREATION AND OTHER DIVERSIONS

Long before the arrival of the white man, the Ute Indians raced their "borrowed" Spanish ponies in the meadows of the valley. The early settlers, not to be outdone, held horse races of their own, and competed with the Utes. History does not report any results, but it is known that the Utes were excellent horsemen.

Walter Devereux and the other landed gentry of early Glenwood Springs considered horse racing against the unwashed cowboys of the day to be somewhat less than genteel. As part of their efforts to civilize the area, they orchestrated construction of a polo field to the south of town. The improvements included not only the field itself, but also a golf course, a grandstand, and a clubhouse. Polo immediately became the "in thing", and teams from as far away as Nebraska came to the valley to compete. The Glenwood

*An overview of Glenwood Springs from the top of Red Mountain, about 1903, showing the polo field in the lower right-hand corner.* (Courtesy of Frontier Historical Society - Schutte Collection)

*Alvin Devereux, captain of the Glenwood Springs Polo Team - about 1902.* (Courtesy of Frontier Historical Society)

*Championship cup won by the Glenwood Springs Polo Club in 1901.* (Courtesy of Frontier Historical Society)

Springs team won three world championships. In need of opponents on a regular basis, they recruited some of the local cowboys, and taught them the game. As it turned out, they got a little more than they bargained for; the cowboys and their agile cutting horses gave them some very stiff competition.

Hunting and fishing have always been popular pastimes in the Glenwood Springs area. The early inhabitants, of course, depended on meat and fish to round out their diets. In more recent years, sport fishing and recreational "harvesting" of big game have brought thousands of sportspersons to the area. Teddy Roosevelt hunted not only bear, but also mountain lion, deer and elk during his visits. The Roaring Fork River and the Frying Pan, one of its subsidiaries, boast some of the finest trout fishing in the country.

Prior to World War II, in the very early days of recreational skiing, ski runs were hacked out of the oak brush on Red Mountain, just to the west of downtown. One of

*Scene from No Name Creek - about 1900.* (Courtesy of Frontier Historical Society)

Colorado's first chair lifts was installed, and an early passenger was tossed out and suffered a concussion. After recovering from a coma and extensive rehabilitation, R. Morris (Buck) Buckmaster went on to be a ski instructor. "Vandy" Vanderhoof and his two sons, John and Don, were instrumental in the development of "Holiday Hill", some 10 miles up Four-Mile Creek. The higher elevation of the new ski area offered a more dependable snowpack. A 3,800 foot rope tow was rigged up, powered by a 1930 Dodge pickup. After a couple of years, Holiday Hill was closed at the insistence of an investor who wanted to develop the former area on Red Mountain. The lower altitude was not conducive to good skiing conditions, and the new Red Mountain area again closed. A smaller area, Mountain Meadows, was built near

*Three feet of fish!* (Courtesy of Frontier Historical Society - Schutte Collection)

the top of Red Mountain, which was accessible by the road which is still visible on the side of the mountain. Two years later, that area also closed. In about 1960, John Higgs purchased much of the land around the former Holiday Hill, formed an investment group, and reopened the area as Sunlight Ski Area. The area has expanded over the intervening years, and now offers not only downhill skiing and snowboarding, but also cross-country skiing, snowshoeing, and snowmobile trails.

The Colorado and the Roaring Fork Rivers provide challenging currents and the occasional stretch of white water rapids for the rafting and kayak enthusiast. Commercial rafting companies now transport several hundred awe-struck tourists down the rivers on a given weekend, but early attempts to navigate the Colorado were fraught with danger. In May of 1956, three men attempted to run the most vicious stretch of Glenwood Canyon water, just below the Shoshone Dam. They were using a war surplus raft, a 25 footer made of heavy black neoprene and canvas. With over 200 spectators watching, they launched the raft. The river grabbed the craft, spun it down Cottonwood Falls, and sucked it un-

*The early days of the Red Mountain ski area.* (Courtesy of Frontier Historical Society - Schutte Collection)

*Holiday Hill Ski Course, at the site of the present Sunlight Ski Complex.* (Courtesy of Frontier Historical Society - Schutte Collection)

der. When the craft was spit back out, it was empty. Two of the men escaped, one with a dislocated shoulder. The third was found a month later, some 30 miles downstream.

*Commercial raft trip on the Colorado River.* (Courtesy of Blue Sky Adventures, Inc.)

In the early days of tourism, guests at the Hotel Colorado or the Hotel Glenwood were entertained with carriage or horseback rides which featured the spectacular scenery of the area. One of the favorites was a ride up Red Canyon south of town to watch the sunset on Mount Sopris. On the return trip, the glow of the fires in the Cardiff coke ovens could be seen. An old Ute Indian trail led from the south side of the river to the summit of Lookout Mountain. It was improved into a bridal path which is now known as the "Boy Scout Trail". An observatory was constructed at the top of the mountain, and was used in 1910 to view Haley's Comet.

Another popular tour was to the Fairy Caves, some 1400 feet from the Hotel Colorado, up Iron Mountain to the north. These stalactite and stalagmite-filled caverns were lit by electric lights, and were accessible by foot or on the back of a burro. A 200 foot tunnel had been dug from the main caves to a smaller cave overlooking the "Canon of the Grand". It was aptly named "Exclamation Point". The caves are quite

*Interior of the Fairy Caves, on Iron Mountain north of the Hotel Colorado.* (Courtesy of Frontier Historical Society)

*"Roughing it" in style!* (Courtesy of Frontier Historical Society)

extensive, the second largest in Colorado. Approximately 7,800 feet of the caves have been surveyed. The attraction was closed to the public in 1917, and has yet to be reopened.

As part of the polo field complex, the Devereux brothers opened the first golf course in the area. That course has long since been replaced with a housing development, but others have taken its place. The city course sits on the hill overlooking the Colorado River from the north, and the Westbank course is surrounded by the homes of the Westbank Subdivision south of town. Rifle and Battlement Mesa offer their own courses to the west, and the new Aspen Glen links, a private course, winds around the luxurious homes in the gated community north of Carbondale.

Then as now, the magnificent fall colors are an attraction to the tourist. The gold of the aspens, the orange and yellow and red of the oak brush paint the high valleys and the south-facing slopes for a few special days each autumn.

The mountains have also drawn a special type of outdoor enthusiast. The hiking and mountain bike trails beckon to the backpacker and the weekend athlete. The Flattops north of town and Four-Mile Park beyond Sunlight Ski area offer endless horizons to the snowmobiler, the horseman, the four-wheeler. The entire area, the mountains, the wilderness, the changing seasons, and the architecture of the town itself draws the photographer to Glenwood Springs.

CHAPTER 13

# "WE WILL NOT FORGET"

The early summer of 1994 ushered in one of the worst fire seasons in memory for the Colorado high country. The previous winter was one of low snowpack, and the spring had been abnormally dry. By early July, a multitude of forest fires were burning on the western slope of Colorado; various firefighting teams had been called in from all over the western states. Forty new fires had been started by lightning in the Bureau of Land Management's Grand Junction District in just the two days prior to July 2, 1994.

At about 6:30 on the evening of July 2, a dry lightning storm blew over the hills to the west of Glenwood Springs. A lone finger of lightning snaked from the clouds and struck a tree almost at the top of a ridge of Storm King Mountain. The tree burst into flame, igniting other trees and brush in the immediate vicinity. The little fire was on a knoll overlooking Interstate 70 and the Colorado River. The wind was from the north, so the only way for it to increase in size was to burn down toward the Colorado. Down is not a natural direction for fire to travel, so it was contained to about three acres. It was under observation, but a fire of that size generated little concern, given the much larger fires in process. The fires which threatened property, or which looked as though they would spread, received priority. By the Fourth of July, the fire had spread to 11 acres, and the local populace began to express a degree of concern. On the afternoon of the 4th, the District sent a crew to deal with it. It was a two and a half hour hike to the fire from the base of the ridge near Interstate 70. The crew arrived at 6:30, and decided to wait until the next morning to begin firefighting efforts.

On the morning of the 5th, a seven person crew from the BLM and the Forest Service hiked to the fire, cleared a landing area for a helicopter, and began a fireline. There

*The Prineville Hotshots prepare to fight the Storm King fire.* (Courtesy of Glenwood Post)

was a drop of fire retardent, or "slurry", during the day. That evening, the crew left the site of the fire to repair their equipment, and eight smokejumpers parachuted into the area and continued to work on firelines until about midnight. They were forced to construct new firelines further down the mountain, as the fire had by then overrun the original lines. The following morning, they were joined by the BLM/Forest Service crew and eight more smokejumpers. Later in the day, Hotshot Crew members from Prineville, Oregon arrived on the scene, and the entire contingent worked on building firelines to halt the advances of the now raging fire.

As the 6th of July wore on, the fire consumed more and more of the pinon pine, cedar, and Gambel oak which covered the steep slopes of Storm King Mountain. There were more air drops of water and slurry, but the fire shrugged them off and continued its rampage. The massed firefighters would gain precious ground, only to be forced back by another flare-up. By that time the forces on the mountain included BLM personnel, Forest Service firefighters,

*A helitack helicopter and crew member - Storm King Mountain in the background.* (Courtesy of Glenwood Post)

smokejumpers from several western states, Helitack crew members, and the Hotshots. Some of America's finest young firefighters, both male and female, faced a fire that was out of control, and which was about to become an inferno.

At about 3:20 PM on the 6th, a cold front moved in. The winds had been bad all along, and a fire of any size will create its own winds, but the weather front brought with it the makings of a disaster. The fire was by that time quite extensive, so there were personnel in several different locations. When the fierce new winds caught the fire, the steep drainage on the west side of Storm King literally exploded. A wall of fire blasted up the hill with incredible speed, covering some 1900 feet in two minutes. Twelve firefighters were overrun by the flames as they tried to make it to the ridge line, and two others were trapped as they tried to escape along that same ridge.

It is to these fourteen courageous young people that Storm King Mountain will always belong.

It was not possible for the residents of Glenwood Springs to know what was happening up on the mountain on the

*Firefighters search for any sign of life on the mountain after the blowup.* (Courtesy of Glenwood Post)

afternoon of July 6, 1994. It was only obvious that something extraordinary was in process. The sun was all but blocked out by the billowing clouds of brownish-gray smoke. The light took on an eerie quality, and flakes of gray ash fell over the entire area. The ponderous shapes of the slurry bombers, the quicker spotter planes, and the insect-like helicopters appeared and disappeared in the normally quiet skies over Glenwood. The homeowners in the western part of West Glenwood played garden hoses on their roofs as they watched the fire advance ever closer to the edge of town. Travelers and commuters creeping along Interstate 70 west of Glenwood saw tongues of fire reaching down the drainages on the south side of Storm King Mountain. At about 4:30, they saw the entire top of the mountain go up. It resembled a gigantic volcanic eruption, the flames and smoke shooting straight up with unimaginable force. The knowledge that there were people up there was chilling.

When the rumors started flying, the word came down that 50 firefighters were missing, then 30, and finally 14. That figure, unfortunately, proved to be accurate. Four

*Granite crosses awaiting installation on the mountain.* (Courtesy of Glenwood Post)

young women and ten young men died in the performance of their jobs, the fighting of wildfires and the protection of the lives and property of others. The realization of the tragedy hit the residents of Glenwood Springs like a fist. Glenwood is, in many ways, a small town. It has had its own share of disasters and untimely deaths. When it was learned that nine of the hotshots had come from another small town, Prineville, Oregon, Glenwood Springs felt an immediate kinship. The day after the blowup, the City Council created the Storm King 14 Monument Committee. The committee consisted of 14 members, including the Glenwood Springs Mayor, representatives from the Forest Service and from the BLM, local artists, and others who felt that they could make a contribution. Each of the committee members adopted one of the families of the fallen firefighters. They did their best to help the family members through the terrible days following the catastrophe. As one member said, "I wanted to do something. I wanted to say something in some way."

The committee also met weekly to bring about the establishment of a memorial to the 14. Two Rivers Park, a green expanse between Interstate 70 and the Colorado River was chosen as the site of the monument. The park is within the city which the firefighters were working to save, but it commands a clear view of Storm King Mountain. The committee called for entries for the design of the monument, and Joyce Killebrew of Sedona, Arizona was chosen. Ms. Killebrew herself worked with the Forest Service for some 20 years as a fire lookout and firefighter. Her life-size bronze sculpture depicts a smokejumper, a helitack crew member and a hotshot — two men and a woman. It sits atop a marble base in the west end of Two Rivers Park. Surrounding the monument are 14 boulders, each with a picture and a brief biography of one of the fallen firefighters.

A rough footpath up the west side of Storm King Mountain was widened and improved by volunteers. Originally used by the families of the victims to reach the sites where the bodies were found, the trail was deliberately left steep and rugged; it was felt that visitors to the site should gain some idea of the terrain faced by the firefighters. The developed path leads to an observation point from which may be seen the granite crosses which have been erected, one for each of the 14.

The trail may be found by traveling west on Interstate 70 to the Canyon Creek exit. About a half mile back east on the frontage road, there is a small parking area. At the trailhead, there is explanatory signage with a diagram of the fire area and information on the 14 firefighters. Hiking shoes, water, and good lungs are recommended. It is not an easy climb, in more ways than one.

*Bronze monument at the west end of Two Rivers Park.* (Photo by the author)

CHAPTER 14

# HIGHS AND LOWS

In the period of its existence, Glenwood Springs has experienced extraordinary highs and crushing lows. Many of these swings followed similar flows in the attitude or economy of the state, the country, or the world. Other occurrences, whether good or bad, were unique to Glenwood.

As we have seen, the late 1880's saw a period of rapid, almost unbelievable growth in building, amenities, and population. This dynamic progress continued into the early 1890's, with the completion of the Hotel Colorado. For the Devereux's and many of the newly wealthy who frequented the new hotel and the other comforts of the spa, it was truly an era of gracious living. Even the silver panic of 1893, after the United States Government abandoned silver as backing for its currency, did not immediately effect the prosperity of Glenwood Springs.

The nature of Glenwood Springs was, however, due to change. Into the early 1900's, the town was still a mixture of opulence, as evidenced by the spa complex, and the old west, epitomized by the ever-present saloons, gambling halls, and brothels. In 1911, Glenwood lost out to Gunnison as the site of a new teacher's college on the western slope. The aforementioned "dens of iniquity" were considered to be unsuitable for young student teachers. In 1912, Colorado outlawed gambling, and prohibition was looming. The character of "Riverfront" was to change forever.

The guest lists at the hotels diminished as the 1914 war blossomed in Europe. Those American businessmen who had the funds to travel were too busy making money off of Europe's misfortunes to spend more than short vacations in the mountains. When the United States entered the war in 1917, many of the young men from the area enlisted and saw service in France. The Denver and Rio Grande tracks were considered to be vulnerable to enemy sabotage, especially through the canyon. The route was deemed valuable for the movement of troops and supplies, so troops were stationed here to guard the tracks, the bridges, and the town in general.

The Roaring Twenties ushered in prohibition, which of course resulted in illegal stills in many of the ravines around town. John Richardson, the owner of the Silver Club, exhibited a great deal of flexibility when the new laws essentially closed down his operation. He became a prohibition agent.

The economic depression that gripped the entire country in the late 1920's had a similar effect on Glenwood Springs. Tourism dropped even further, and demand for coal and farm products declined. Between 1920 and 1930, for the only time in its history, the population of the town dropped.

As the economy of the country slowly turned around, the residents of Glenwood Springs again began looking forward. Frank Kistler, Wyoming oil man, purchased the Hotel Colorado. J. E. Sayre, for whom the park on South Grand Avenue is named, brought his Oklahoma oil money to town, and George Sumers, a New York City investment broker, purchased most of the ghost town of Cardiff. He built a luxurious home for himself and his family, and donated the land near the coke ovens to the city for use as an airport. The little town at the confluence of the Roaring Fork and the Colorado was on the move again.

On December 7, 1941, Pearl Harbor was attacked and the United States was again thrust into a World War. The character of the town changed almost overnight. The Hotel Colorado was converted into a Navy hospital. The Hot Springs Pool and the Vapor Caves were reserved for the use of recuperating military personnel. Towards the end of the war the Civilian Conservation Corps camp, built on the present site of Sayre Park during the Depression, was converted to a prison camp for Nazi Storm Troopers.

*Located in what is now Sayre Park, the Depression-era CCC camp was converted into a prison camp for Nazi Storm Troopers during World War II.* (Courtesy of Frontier Historical Society)

The wartime rationing of gasoline and rubber severely curtailed tourism by automobile, and Glenwood Springs was forced to pull back into itself. Many of the young people who had been offered a taste of the world during the war did not return to Glenwood. The founders of the town were reaching retirement age, and many chose to remain in the area. There were newcomers, but they mostly purchased existing businesses, and few new stores were opened.

The destruction of the Hotel Glenwood by fire in 1945 was followed by a potentially disastrous explosion and fire in 1948 when wholesale oil tanks blew up. According to accounts, only the quick action of the Volunteer Fire Department and the lack of a wind kept the resulting sheets of flame from engulfing most of the town.

Mention has been made elsewhere of disasters in the coal mines of the area and of the tragedy of the fire on Storm King Mountain. Coal mining and firefighting are hazardous occupations, and injury or death, while by no means any less tragic, are not totally unforeseen. It was with a

*Billowing smoke from burning oil tanks which threatened Glenwood Springs in 1945.* (Courtesy of Buzz Zancanella)

great deal of shock, however, that the citizens of Glenwood received the news on December 16, 1985 that the Rocky Mountain Natural Gas Company building had blown up. The office building/warehouse on the south side of the Colorado River was the site of a massive explosion which leveled the building and killed 12 people.

Many Colorado mountain towns have experienced the boom/bust syndrome. Most of these fluctuations in fortune have been the result of the vagrancies of gold or silver mining. However, Glenwood Springs and most of Garfield County took a serious financial hit on "Black Sunday", May 2, 1982. On that date, Exxon Corporation abruptly pulled out of the oil shale operation which they had been operating in the western part of the county. The hundreds of jobs that had been created in an effort to extract usable petroleum from the shale bluffs north and west of Rifle suddenly vanished. A flurry of business closures and not a few bankruptcies followed the pullout by the oil giant.

Colorado Mountain College, located in the south side of Spring Valley southeast of town, has provided employment and educational opportunities for valley residents. In addition, it offers a variety of classes to students from all over the world. The College headquarters are now located in downtown Glenwood, and the Blake Street Center specializes in vocational and adult education.

During the 1990's, the Glenwood Springs Chamber Resort Association and individual businesses have concentrated on promoting Glenwood Springs as a tourist Mecca. The recreational opportunities of the forests, the rivers, and the mountains attract hunters, fishermen, mountain bikers, hikers, and all sorts of other outdoor enthusiasts. Interestingly, however, the amenities that were promoted by Walter Devereux, such as the giant pool, the vapor caves, and the magnificent scenery, are among the major offerings mentioned in today's advertising.

CHAPTER 15

# GLENWOOD CANYON

The rock layers in Glenwood Canyon have been in the process of forming since the surface of the Earth cooled. In the billions of years since, no one has a clue how many times the seas covered the area, only to be forced away again by rock upthrusts. Some of these cataclysmic events were the result of the shifting of the tectonic plates. These plates underlay both the oceans and the continents and float on the liquid magma, the molten rock, which makes up the Earth's core. Each of the plates is in constant, if slow, movement. If one of the plates rides up over the edge of another, or if two of them collide, the result is a dramatic uplift. Most of the existing mountain ranges are the result of these movements.

Other massive formations have been created through volcanic activity. When the underlying magma forces its way upwards through the overlying layers, it solidifies, building upon itself. The accompanying ash and cinders build up in layers many feet deep, eventually solidifying and adding dimension to the landscape. Other mountainous regions have been formed by volcanic intrusions, the raising of the overlying terrain by the pressure of molten rock which never reaches the surface.

Long before the first one celled creatures appeared in the primordial seas, a number of mountain ranges had been formed and in turn were worn down by the irresistible forces of wind and water. As each of them gradually wore away, they left evidence of their existence in the form of rock layers. The sand and sediment washed down and settled, awaiting the next intrusion of sea water. The seas themselves produced their own layers. Once the first life forms did appear, they added their tiny shells and skeletons to the mix. After the next uplift, the whole process began again.

Over the billions of years the resultant rock layers were broken, pushed up, tilted, twisted, and again worn down.

Each cycle left its mark in the different textures and colors of rock. Some were hard and resistant to the forces of erosion, forming shelves and tilted walls. Some were soft, breaking away to create caves and spalls. Eventually, they all yielded to gravity.

Some 300 million years ago, a massive upthrust cracked the seabed covering what was to become Colorado. The Ancestral Rockies pushed skywards, reaching perhaps 35,000 feet in elevation. As they wore away, they deposited red sand over Nebraska, Kansas, much of Utah, and of course, Colorado. The sediment piled up thousands of feet thick in places, covering the older layers. Later, the seas came once more, covering everything. They in turn slowly receded, leaving huge swamps filled with primitive plant life, bizarre amphibians, and giant dragonflies. The coal seams that underlay many of the mountains to the south and west of Glenwood Canyon are the result of those ancient swamps.

Roughly 240 million years after the formation of the Ancestral Rockies, there was a final uplift. Again the rocks thrust into the air, forming the basis for our present day Rocky Mountains. They were of course much higher than they are today, but that was not to last. As the new peaks caught the moisture-laden clouds sweeping eastward, they collected deep deposits of snow and ice.

As the seasons changed and the weather warmed, the snowmelt water cascaded downwards, following always the path of least resistance. As the droplets became streams and the streams became rivers, the water picked up and carried any loose material with it. The small pebbles within the rushing water were abrasive, scratching and eventually wearing the rock over which it flowed. The heavier the flow of water, the bigger the pieces of rock carried with it. With the variance in weather, a waterway which carried only a trickle during the frozen winters could later become a raging torrent, carrying many tons of water, boulders, and trees. Such a rush of material can displace an astounding amount

*Spectacular "Book Cliffs" in the eastern section of Glenwood Canyon.*
(Courtesy of Al Maggard)

of rock in a short time. Even so, it took the Colorado River most of the last 60 million years to cut through the billion or so years of history which makes up Glenwood Canyon.

As the river did its work, it carved a steep, V-shaped cut through the White River Plateau. While the water found an easy path down through the canyon, animals, and later man, did not. The Paleo-Indians, the first human beings to see this part of the world, left little trace of any sort of habitation in the canyon. What little evidence has been found was concentrated at the more accessible east end. The Ute Indians controlled much of Colorado and Utah for hundreds of years, but they preferred to bypass the rushing waters and sheer rock walls.

When the white man came to the area in search of silver and gold, they initially took the lead of the rivers and the Indians by following the path of least resistance. They too followed the valley of the Eagle River westward until it merged with the Grand River, later to be named the Colorado River. Not far to the west of the confluence of the two rivers, the Grand disappeared into an obviously impassable canyon. The prospectors then veered south to cross 8,000 foot Cottonwood Pass to the area of Mount Sopris, or north to the Flattops, the 10,000 foot high country of the White River Plateau. There was, after all, little incentive for anyone to endure the danger and the monumental amount of work which would be involved in pounding any sort of a path through the canyon. The only thing at the west end of the Grand River Canyon worthy of note was a handful of geothermal springs which had been used by the Utes for some centuries. The action was elsewhere.

By the late 1870's, Leadville was the home of some 40,000 souls, drawn there by the lure of silver. Aspen was heating up for the same reason, and there were rumors of promising rock formations at Carbonate, a tent city high up in the Flattops. Such was the excitement over the rumors that the little town was actually platted, streets were named, and Carbonate became the county seat of Garfield County. Little "paydirt" was found at Carbonate, but there was enough activity to cause the building of a toll road down past Windy Point to the area of the Yampah Springs. Even then, access to the road to Aspen was more important than access to the hot springs and the few tents or dugouts tucked away at the west end of the canyon.

Just as the ambitions of Walter Devereux were instrumental in the development of the Yampah Hot Springs, those same ambitions were the driving force behind the first penetration of the Grand River Canyon. The development of the coal mines, the increases in ranching and farming, and the desires of the Devereux brothers to open their new spa to the world all cried out for a railroad. Any railroad would do. It mattered not from which direction it came. That being the case, the Colorado Midland began laying

tracks toward the Roa
had become Defiance, a
ern began the daunting ta
River Canyon from the eas

The efforts of the Midla
actually the first attempts to la
Springs. In 1885, the Burling
the area between the Yampah Sp
the first major creek inside the wes
started construction on a roadbed an
side of the canyon, but wound up aba

A race developed between the Midla &RGW. The rich coal fields awaited the victor, re than just pride was at stake. The D&RGW crew tore into the south wall of the canyon, with little concern for anything other than creating a railbed capable of handling both standard and narrow gauge track. It was obvious by that time that the wider standard gauge was the coming thing, but the rail equipment that serviced the mines was all narrow gauge, so they were taking no chances. The pick and the shovel, the rock drill and blasting powder were the instruments with which the crew moved an amazing amount of rock.

All of this activity took place many years before the word "environmentalist" was coined. As far as we know, no one showed up to protest the destruction of the plant life, the ancient rock, and anything else that got in the way of the workmen. Had anyone done so, they probably would have been summarily tossed into the river along with the loose rock that was created in the "building" process. In those days, the emphasis was on getting the job done, on creating a passageway from one place to another. Little or no thought was given to aesthetics. That attitude was likely efficient, but it did serve to seriously scar the previously untouched canyon.

One feature does, however, speak to a sense of craftsmanship by at least one segment of the D&RGW crew. In places near the center of the canyon, it was necessary to

*Avalanche in Glenwood Canyon, 1899.* (Courtesy of Frontier Historical Society)

construct retaining walls to support the railbed or to keep the canyon walls from crumbling onto the tracks. Italian stone masons, with the assistance of Chinese and Mexican laborers, created several walls of closely fitted rocks to accomplish this. The walls still stand today, still support the massive weight of the rail traffic, without the benefit of mortar. The walls were "dry-laid", stacked and fitted so well that they may still be seen under and above the tracks on the south wall of the canyon.

The D&RGW won the race, pulling into Glenwood Springs through the just-completed Jackson Tunnel on the evening of October 5, 1887. The Midland tracks reached Glenwood Springs on December 12 of the same year. With two railroads from the east now reaching the little town, the self-styled "Resort City of the West", the intended playground of the wealthy created by the Devereuxs, was at last open to the outside world. The city of Glenwood Springs, by 1888, grew to a population of 2,500.

With the Grand River Canyon now echoing with the rumble of train travel, it was only a matter of time before someone attempted a road through the same narrow gorge.

*Construction of the Taylor State Road through Glenwood Canyon - 1901.*
(Courtesy of Frontier Historical Society)

In 1890, Henry Morrow, using the original Burlington Railroad survey as a jumping-off point, hacked and blasted a rugged wagon road along the north side of the river. Some crude paths had been carved out over the years between the major creeks which cascaded down the sides of the canyon. Morrow connected these trails for the first time. Like the construction of the railroad, it was no easy task to displace enough rock to create even the one-lane track. Again, Morrow and his workmen had little concern for the vegetation or for the ancient rock formations. The completed trail was dangerous even to foot traffic, susceptible to flooding, rock falls and snow slides, but it was used by freight wagons, pack trains, and even a few stagecoach drivers with more courage than intellect.

*Car on the Taylor State Road through Glenwood Canyon - note the width of the road.* (Courtesy of Frontier Historical Society - Schutte Collection)

State Senator Edward T. Taylor represented the Glenwood Springs area for over 50 years. Recognizing the need for a decent wagon road through the canyon, he succeeded in pushing through an appropriation of $40,000 to build a wagon road from Denver to Grand Junction. The project, completed in 1902, wound up costing some $60,000, half of which was spent in "the canyon east of Glenwood Springs". The May 17, 1902 edition of the *Glenwood Post* quoted A. J. McCune, the designer of the project: "Over a great portion, the road was cut out of solid rock, and as some factitious wag has said, there wasn't a bushel of dirt in the 20 miles." The paper praised H. B. Morrell, the contractor for the road. In places, according to the reporter, it was necessary for the workmen to be lowered from the overhanging cliffs to drill the holes for blasting the roadway.

*The Taylor State Road in Glenwood Canyon, about 1910, during low water. Note the fill which had been dumped in the river from both railroad and highway construction.* (Courtesy of Frontier Historical Society - Schutte Collection)

In a very unusual move for the turn of the century, the original plans for the Taylor State Road specified that wherever possible, the trees and shrubs were to be left undisturbed; the natural beauty was to be preserved. It was one of the first road building projects to carry such a proviso. Undoubtedly the plans came as somewhat of a surprise to the workers, who were accustomed to simply clearing a roadbed and going on from there. Of course, there is some doubt as to how carefully the regulations were carried out. They may have had the best of intentions, but the standards of "environmental awareness" were obviously somewhat loose in those days.

In 1902, a gentleman named W. W. Price drove one of the new-fangled automobiles from Colorado Springs to

Leadville, then over Tennessee Pass and through the just-completed canyon road to Glenwood Springs. There, to the great annoyance of the populace, he proceeded to parade his "gas buggy" up and down Grand Avenue, "endangering people's lives by frightening their horses".

In 1906, race driver Barney Oldlfield made a record coast to coast run, thoughtfully including the Taylor State Road through the canyon in his itinerary. History does not report what he thought of the condition of the road.

The white man had now pushed both a railroad and a crude but serviceable wagon road through the canyon which was once thought to be impassable. However, they were not yet done. There was a resource in the canyon that attracted the attention of the Colorado Power and Irrigation Company. That resource was the mighty Colorado River, then known as the Grand. When one thinks of hydroelectric power, huge dams such as Hoover Dam at Lake Mead, or the Glen Canyon Dam which holds back the waters of Lake Powell come to mind. However, the dependable, powerful flow of water through Glenwood Canyon provided the power necessary to generate significant amounts of electricity.

Like all of the other projects which man has attempted in the canyon, the building of the Shoshone Hydroelectric Complex presented the designers and engineers with some unique challenges. The initial plans were drawn in 1903, and construction was begun in December, 1906. The relatively low volume of water flow in the dead of winter aided the workmen a great deal in the construction of Shoshone Dam.

The Shoshone Complex is somewhat unique in that electricity is not generated in the usual way. That is, most hydroelectric power comes from the force of water flowing through or around a dam. In the case of the Shoshone Plant, the dam diverts the water from the river bed into a tunnel. This tunnel is one of the most unusual features of the system. It enters the north wall of the canyon and continues

12,700 feet or 2.3 miles westward, following the natural slope of the canyon itself. It was drilled and blasted through solid granite. The interior dimensions of the bore are 11 by 16 feet, with a carrying capacity of 1,250 cubic feet of water per second. At the lower end of the tunnel, the deluge of water turns two giant turbines. They in turn power generators which have produced power to the western slope of Colorado since the completion of the plant in 1910.

Because the Taylor State Road was still rough and subject to vagrancies of the weather, a construction camp was set up in the canyon. It was called Shoshone, and housed over 1,000 men, some with their families. It became a small city with a post office, a company store, a commissary, a

*The Shoshone Rapids in Glenwood Canyon, prior to the construction of the dam.* (Courtesy of Frontier Historical Society)

*The Shoshone Power Plant, in 1907. The large building to the right was a boarding house; small houses to the left were homes of managers .* (Courtesy of Frontier Historical Society)

hospital, apartments, and even a school for the workmen's children. In addition, there were warehouses, offices, and a railroad depot. Many of the supplies needed in the construction were brought in by the D&RGW.

The original plans called for the Shoshone Plant to be a temporary structure, to be used only until the tunnel could be extended further down the river, and another, larger plant could be constructed there. However, the economic depression of 1907 helped to permanently delay those plans, and the "temporary" steel and sheet metal facility still stands.

As with the construction of the railroad and to a lesser extent the Taylor State Road, little heed was paid to the environment in the building of the Shoshone Power Plant. The resulting scars have been covered somewhat by vegetation and by the natural mineral staining of the rock, but they have never totally healed.

As early as 1902, groups such as the Colorado Auto Club, an organization of 42 automobile owners in Denver, began campaigning for better roads throughout the state. It was not until 1909 that the first highway commission was formed, with the princely sum of $56,000 in funding. It was, however, a start. In 1913, $75,000 was appropriated to improve the road through “the Canyon of the Grand”, as it was still known, and it was designated as part of the Pikes Peak Ocean-to-Ocean Highway in 1914. Even so, travelers approaching the canyon in October of 1914 were greeted by a sign stating that the Glenwood Canyon road was “closed for the winter”.

In the late 1930's, Edward T. Taylor, by now a U. S. Congressman, sponsored legislation for a federal highway from the Kansas border to Utah. As part of that project, $1.5 million was designated for the improvement of the road through Glenwood Canyon, now US Highway 40. The roadway was

*The eastern entrance to "Glenwood Canon," about 1955.* (Courtesy of Al Maggard)

widened to 29 feet, with 25 feet of pavement and two feet of gravel shoulder on each side. In addition, many turnouts and picnic and parking areas were included in the design. The canyon highway became part of U.S. Highway 6 & 24 in 1938. The Glenwood Canyon road was becoming more and more of a scenic attraction with the increases in vehicular traffic. However, its 57 curves, many of them blind, contributed to mounting accident rates.

The outbreak of World War II had a profound effect on Glenwood Canyon. What had been a pleasant, if unsafe passage through magnificent cliffs became a vital transportation corridor for the military. In addition, the war-time rationing of rubber and gasoline severely curtailed recreational travel. Most of the maintenance during this period was done by Army and Navy personnel, and consisted largely of removing fallen rocks from the roadway.

The end of the war saw the birth of the interstate highway system, with four or more lanes of traffic, higher speed limits, and a lack of stop lights or signs to impede the increasing flow of automobile and truck traffic. In the period from the early 50s to the middle 70s the wide lanes of pavement crept across the United States, linking some towns and cities, bypassing others. As might be expected, Colorado presented some interesting challenges to the designers and builders of the interstates. Naturally, the easy parts were done first. The eastern slope of the state, with its major metropolitan centers and resultant population, received the most attention. By the middle of 1975, Interstate 25 was completed from the Wyoming line south through Denver and Colorado Springs to the New Mexico border. I-76 was all but complete from Denver to the Nebraska border, and all but 6 miles of I-70 were open from Denver to Kansas. The four-lane highway was creeping westward from the outskirts of Denver toward the Continental Divide. The Eisenhower Tunnel, the first of two bores which bypass Loveland Pass, had been completed. Perhaps not surprisingly, the 20 or so miles which included Glenwood Canyon were put far back on the burner.

There was an understandable concern from many quarters regarding the feasibility, even the possibility, of building a four lane highway through Glenwood Canyon. It was an exceptionally scenic canyon which, in many places, was barely wide enough to contain the river, the railroad, and a narrow two-lane road. The initial reactions were varied. Some looked at the still-healing wounds from the turn of the century railway and road construction and shuddered, envisioning great devastation, imagining the everlasting ruin of their beloved canyon. There was a great cry for the interstate system to bypass Glenwood Canyon entirely, to send the route over Cottonwood Pass or up over the Flattops. Some sarcastically suggested running the river through a massive culvert, and just paving over it. The stage was set for one of the most amazing series of meetings, studies, arguments, and compromises known to man.

Floyd Diemoz is a member of one of the pioneer families of the Roaring Fork Valley, and except for a period during and just after World War II, a lifelong resident. He has been involved in concerned public input on highway department activities since the 1963 hearings on the twin tunnels at the west end of the canyon. In July, 1965, he wrote a letter to the editor of the *Glenwood Post,* stating that the decisions whether the Colorado River would run through town within its natural banks or within concrete retaining walls, whether the town would be viewed through trees and grass or through a chain-link fence, would reside not with the highway department, but with the residents of Glenwood Springs. True to his word, Diemoz was in the forefront when a citizen's committee was formed to provide input on the possible interstate construction through the canyon.

The highway department, the citizen's advisory committee, several environmental groups, and many others provided input on the project. Fairly early in the proceedings, first the Flattops route and then the Cottonwood Pass route were shot down as possibilities. The Flattops route would take the road to 10,000 feet in elevation, with the resultant weather-related problems, and extend the route some 42 miles. It was estimated that building the road over the White River Plateau would increase the cost by a factor of five. Likewise, Cottonwood Pass would require more right-of-way procurement and steep grades at high altitudes, very similar to Vail Pass. It was decided that adding a third high mountain pass to the interstate route through Colorado was not an attractive alternative.

It therefore came down to Glenwood Canyon. As difficult, as expensive, as impossible as it seemed, the magnificent canyon was to be subjected to the construction of a modern four lane highway from one end to the other. Not only that, but the designers of the roadway were charged with the creation of rest areas, recreational access to the creeks and the river, and a walking/bike path for the entire length of the canyon. They were also to accomplish all of the above with little or no damage to the scenic beauty of the existing vegetation or the 2,000 foot walls of ancient rock. There were many who considered the task to be simply impossible.

Floyd Diemoz, Jim Rose, Ed Mulhall, and Jerry Brown, all members of the transportation committee of the Glenwood Springs Chamber of Commerce, produced a 22 minute film which investigated the three alternative routes. The film strongly recommended Glenwood Canyon as the only feasible route. It featured several shots of scars caused by former construction in the canyon to emphasize the fact that standard highway construction techniques would simply not be acceptable. The film then went on to illustrate Italian road-building techniques that employed elevated spans of roadway well above the native rock and vegetation.

The initial reactions to the idea of sending one or both sides of the new highway skyward varied from disbelief to horror. The concept of motor homes and 18-wheelers blasting by on some sort of an aerial ribbon of roadway while chipmunks played and families devoured picnic lunches below was just too close to science fiction for many people to swallow. Not only that, but many of the skeptics were familiar with the normal operating procedures of building a highway. They had seen the bulldozers at work, leaving in their wake wide swaths of bare dirt. That was, after all, the logical way to begin a highway; clear out everything in the path of the proposed road and go from there. At least that's how it was done in the good old days. Well, said the environmentalists, not this time!

There were as many opinions as there were factions. Colorado's Environmental Commission stated that it would be impossible to build a four lane highway without total destruction of the canyon and the recreational usage of it. The road building industry said that the only sensible method of building a road was through the use of "cut and fill", the technology which had earlier produced the barren slopes to the north of the frontage road between Glenwood Springs and West Glenwood. The more hard-core of the environmentalists still insisted that Glenwood Canyon was no place for any kind of an interstate highway. In the middle of it all stood those who said, to quote Floyd Diemoz again, "Yes, we can do it. We can be careful. We can be bold and innovative. Yes, we can do it right."

Two architects, both of whom have since been called "inspired designers", were given the challenge of conceptualizing a highway design that would successfully match the art of nature with the engineering of man. They were Joseph Passonneau from Washington, D. C., and Edgardo Contini from Los Angeles. In John Haley's excellent book on Glenwood Canyon, *"Wooing a Harsh Mistress: Glenwood Canyon's Highway Odyssey"*, he quotes Contini; "It was not a matter of designing a highway, or it was not a matter of creating a recreational environment. It was the issue of resolving very real, conflicting demands. The canyon is a very restricted and very delicate and very sensitive environment. The difficulty was how to reconcile the scale of the highway with the scale of the canyon itself."

*Construction of the bridge near the Shoshone Power Plant.* (Courtesy of Casey Peter, Colorado Department of Transportation)

For the next several years the two architects, along with the engineers from other design firms, Colorado Department of Highways engineers, and the citizen's advisory committee, literally designed the canyon highway inch by inch. Ralph Trapani, the Colorado Department of Transportation Project Manager, worked closely with the various groups, providing a liaison between them. As the design phase progressed, the courts heard a lawsuit which had been filed on behalf of several environmental and river sports groups. The plaintiffs sought to halt construction in the canyon, citing serious environmental concerns. In ruling against them, the judge spoke to the assurances by the defendants that the canyon project would result in actual restoration of the canyon, rather than adding to the scars inflicted by earlier construction.

Construction actually commenced in 1980, beginning at both the east and west ends of the canyon, and progressing toward the middle, the more difficult areas. The work was planned to take 12 years. Some 40 separate contracts were awarded. The cost estimates for the total project were then $306 million, up from the 1976 figure of $166 million.

*Tensioning ducts to be covered with concrete and tightened to create the road surface.* (Courtesy of Casey Peter, Colorado Department of Transportation)

One of the major concerns prior to the construction phase was the interruption of traffic. It had been decided that a Cottonwood Pass detour was out of the question, due to the cost considerations that disqualified it as a potential route for the interstate. By the same token, delays of several hours, a real possibility given the technical nature of the construction, were unacceptable. The solution, which ultimately saved time for the contractors, held traffic delays to 30 minutes, and won an achievement award from the Institute of Transportation Engineers, was a system of pilot cars. The radio-equipped cars, which led single lane traffic through and past the construction activity, allowed the contractors to continue working in the other lane. During the construction period, there were no traffic related deaths or serious injuries.

*Hanging Lake, high on the north wall of Glenwood Canyon* . (Courtesy of Frontier Historical Society)

Since its discovery, there has been one feature of Glenwood Canyon, one strange geological phenomenon, one jewel-like scenic wonder, that has demanded attention. That feature is Hanging Lake. Created by a geologic fault perhaps thousands of years ago, Hanging Lake does in fact hang from the side of the north wall of the canyon. The rim of the lake has been built up from the limestone in the water, and is quite fragile. It is a small, startlingly blue acre and a half of water accessible by one of Colorado's most used hiking trails. The trail is steep, but the reward at the end is well worth the effort. Hanging lake is home to brook trout, and is fed by a lacy waterfall. Because of that, there was real concern about the design of the highway in that area. There was obviously need of a parking area, but the major worry was the traffic noise from a four-lane interstate highway almost directly beneath the lake.

The solution to this apprehension took several forms. First, all four lanes of the interstate were moved to the south side of the river. This allowed plenty of room for access roads, parking area, rest area, and a walking/bike trail to

*The falls at Hanging Lake.* (Courtesy of Frontier Historical Society - Schutte Collection)

the trailhead. Second, the lanes were imbedded in what have become known as the Hanging Lake tunnels, twin bores through the granite on the south wall. The granite was strong enough to allow the use of the natural arch of the tunnels to support themselves. Rock bolts were added for additional security, and the interior was finished with a thin concrete lining and ceramic tiles. The tunnels are some 4,000 feet long.

To the casual observer, the twin tunnels are just that. They sport attractively curved entrance "barrels", and are well-lit and free of the exhaust haze that lingers in many highway tunnels. However, many drivers have been startled

*The east portals of the Hanging Lake Tunnels.* (Courtesy of Casey Peter, Colorado Department of Transportation)

to see a highway department vehicle slow and then disappear into the wall of the tunnel. Upon closer inspection, giant four-part doors can be spotted in the walls. When they are opened, the traveler can catch a glimpse of some of the inner workings of these amazing underground passages. The Hanging Lake tunnels are the nerve center of the entire canyon. They possess technology which is found nowhere else in the United States. The ground level, the level which may occasionally be spotted through the open doors, contains fire trucks, a tunnel washing vehicle, and a short wheel base tow truck that is capable of moving any vehicle which might happen by. This level also contains full support facilities for the various vehicles.

That is only the base, if you will, of the iceberg. The tunnels cut across Cinnamon Creek, a valley on the south side of the canyon. The engineers took advantage of the natural terrain to build a four story building which has become the command center of the tunnel and of the canyon itself. The structure is the tallest building in Garfield County. It is so integrated into the landscape, so hidden by

*The control room of Hanging Lake Tunnels* . (Courtesy of Casey Peter, Colorado Department of Transportation)

rock formations and vegetation, that someone might drive through the Hanging Lake tunnels for years, and never be aware of its existence. A small portion of the building may be glimpsed from the walking/bike trail between the Hanging Lake rest area and the Hanging Lake trailhead. The second and third levels of the building house four 300 horsepower fans, which together are capable of moving 240,000 cubic feet of air per minute. In the case of a vehicle fire in one of the bores, the fans can be reversed to exhaust the resultant heat and smoke.

The fourth floor contains the brain center of the tunnels. Under the eyes of human tunnel operators, an impressive bank of computers and a huge wall of television monitors keep track of literally everything that happens, or is likely to happen, in the tunnels or on the tunnel approaches. Sensors check for icy conditions on the bridges of the canyon and on the tunnel approaches. Other sensors check for excessive speed or for over-height vehicles, and activate overhead message signs. Perhaps most amazingly, each vehicle that enters the tunnels is sensed by the computers and tracked. If the vehicle does not leave the tunnel within a reasonable time, given its speed, the computers notify an operator. If the "Incident Detection and Management System" detects anything out of the ordinary, such as a stalled vehicle, an accident, a fire, or other anomaly, it not only mentions it to the operator, but also gives him or her a menu of possible choices of action. Once the operator makes a selection, the computers then activate it.

It is doubtful the systems in the tunnels will fail due to a power outage. Both Public Service Company of Colorado and Holy Cross Electric provide electrical service to the tunnels. In addition, the utility companies are backed up by an emergency generator, which is backed up by huge storage batteries.

Whereas most tunnels are the enemy of radio reception, the Hanging Lake tunnels are again the exception. They are equipped with an AM-FM rebroadcast system that allows motorists to continue listening to their favorite station. Not only that, but controllers may communicate with the vehicles in the tunnel in case of an emergency, regardless of the radio station to which the motorist is listening. The tunnel complex has been called the "Intelligent Highway of the Future" with good reason.

While the majority of the technical marvels of the Hanging Lake tunnels are hidden from view, the remainder of the canyon highway is necessarily open to inspection. The smooth visual flow of the traffic lanes from one end of the canyon to the other hides the fact that there are actually four different types of construction involved in the highway. The decision to use each method in its own particular area was based on existing terrain and environment, aesthetic values, and cost. The four classifications of girders which make up the highway include cast-in-place concrete box girders, steel box girders, steel plate girders, and precast segmental box girders. The four types were combined with such planning and skill that there are no obvious transitions from one to the other. The canyon highway is a blending of

*The westbound lanes hug the canyon wall as eastbound traffic rises toward the French Creek viaduct*. (Courtesy of Casey Peter, Colorado Department of Transportation)

normal ground level roadway, viaducts, and bridges. There are some 40 total above-grade structures, ranging from 100 feet in length to over 7,000 feet. Some of the viaducts and bridges were constructed for the normal uses, such as crossing the rivers of creeks, but many of them were designed simply to protect the fragile environment.

Certain of the narrower parts of the canyon demanded rather special handling, to avoid damage to the rock and vegetation. At those locations, the higher, westbound lanes were constructed by casting a series of piers or towers in place, and then using a French-made gantry to position precast girders. The self-propelled gantry "walked" along from tower to tower, placing the girders, which were held in place with epoxy and tensioning rods. After finishing a section, the gantry would move on to the next pier and begin the process anew. The girders for this section were cast in Eagle, a town 20 miles to the east.

While a great deal of the attractiveness of the finished highway stems from the design of the construction itself,

*The elevated gantry at work in Glenwood Canyon as traffic continues to move below.* (Courtesy of Casey Peter, Colorado Department of Transportation)

much credit must be given to the crews who did the minimal blasting that took place in the interstate construction. Where many other highway rock cuts show the vertical marks of drilling holes, the Glenwood Canyon crews consulted with geologists, then set their charges to fracture the rock along existing cracks. This method resulted in a much more natural appearance to the new walls. Where necessary, the newly exposed rock was stained to match the natural weathering and lichen patches. The rocks were so artfully colored that it is all but impossible to pick out the stained areas.

To emphasize their commitment to the existing vegetation in the canyon, the highway department put a "bounty" on certain of the plants which were in harm's way. The

*The viaduct at French Creek, curving aroung 80-foot Douglas fir trees.*
(Courtesy of Casey Peter, Colorado Department of Transportation)

fines for removal or destruction of the named foliage ranged from $30 for a raspberry bush up to $22,000 for a Douglas Fir tree. The removal of some plants was unavoidable, but some 180,000 new ones were added during and after construction. At French Creek, westbound traffic curves between the tops of two 80 foot tall Douglas Firs. A comprehensive study of the canyon flora, combined with test plots, resulted in a better understanding of the planting to be done on slopes or in the shaded areas. A complex irrigation system helped the new plantings become established.

At 10:00 AM on October 14, 1992, a ribbon-cutting ceremony marked the first time in 12 years the motoring public could travel the length of the canyon without the anticipation of delays. It would be another year before all of the signing, cleanup, and landscaping would be completed, but the final link, what would be referred to as the "Crowning Jewel of the Interstate System" was done. The total price tag was some $500 million.

More than ever before, Glenwood Canyon is accessible to the hiker, the bicyclist, the fisherman, the rafter. Four rest areas, at No Name, Grizzly Creek, Hanging Lake, and Bair Ranch offer the motorist sanitary facilities, water, access to the bike trail, information on the canyon, and spectacular scenery. The rest areas are all accessible to the handicapped. Grizzly Creek also provides access to a hiking trail which leads to the Flattops, as well as some excellent stream fishing. The 8 foot wide hiking/bike path which runs the length of the canyon is a delight for runners, walkers, bicyclists, and in-line skaters. It runs next to the river for most of its reach, furnishing probably the most intimate way to experience the canyon.

The fortunate traveler who enters Glenwood Canyon from either end is about to experience two miracles. The first was designed, engineered, and constructed by nature, the second by man.

*East and west bound lanes of Interstate 70 in Glenwood Canyon, a biking/ walking trail, and railroad. Barely visible in the river is a raft.* (Courtesy of Casey Peter, Colorado Department of Transportation)

APPENDIX I

# Map of the Glenwood Springs Area

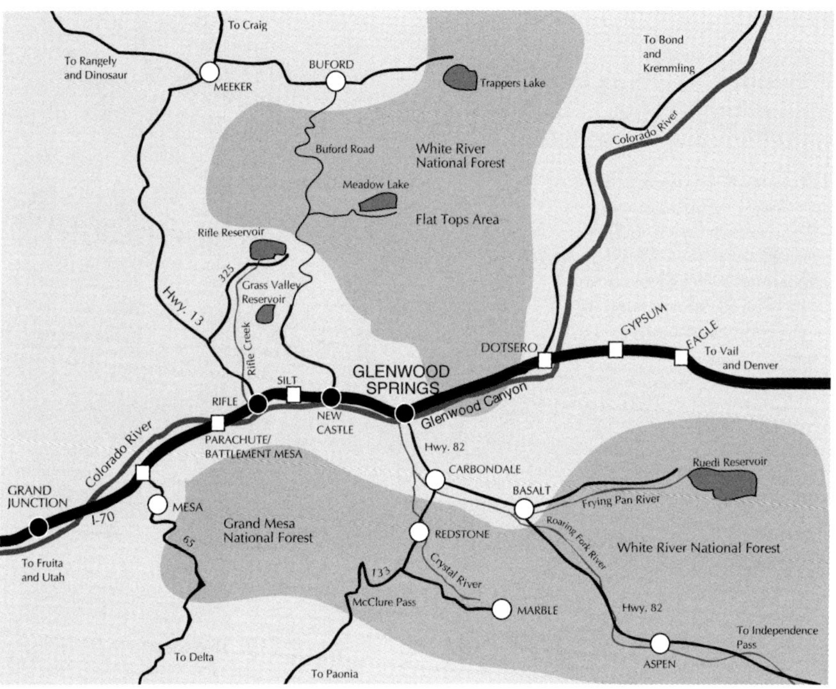


(Courtesy of Glenwood Post)

APPENDIX II

# Map of the City of Glenwood Springs

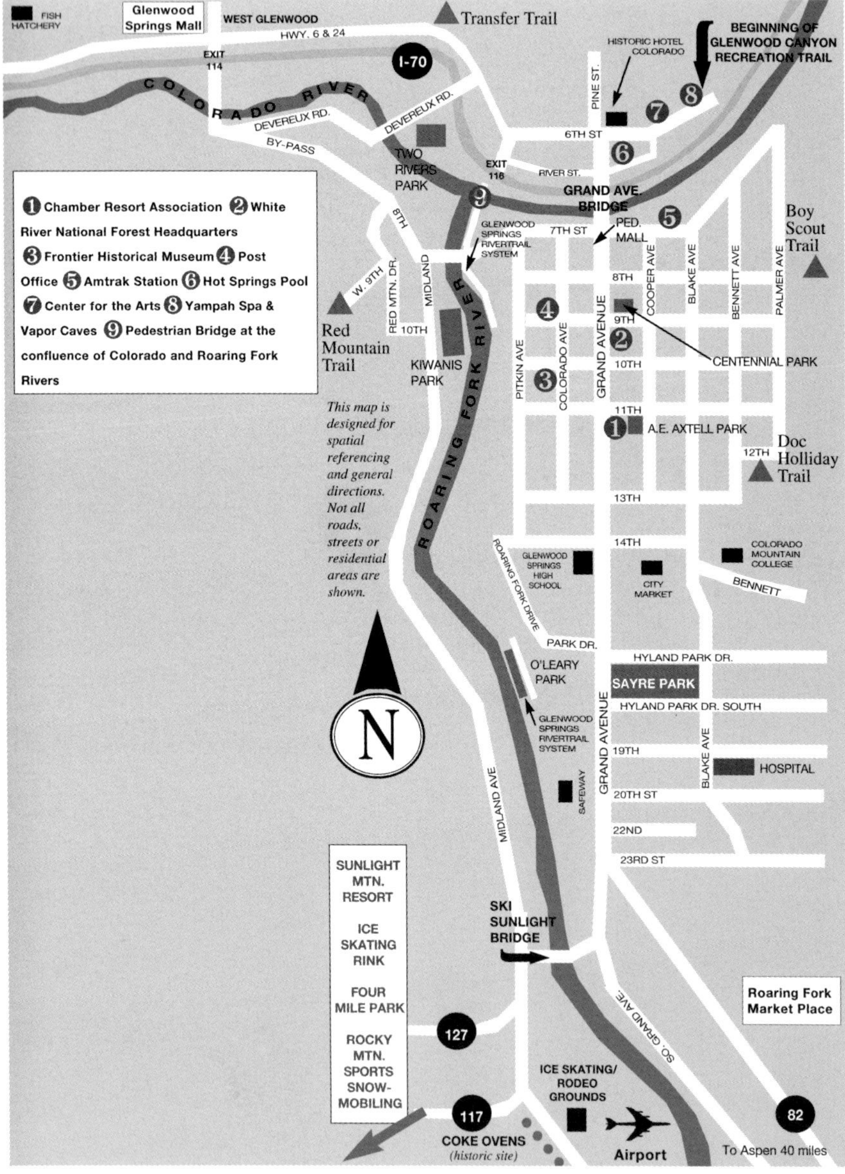


(Courtesy of the Glenwood Springs Chamber of Commerce)

# BIBLIOGRAPHY

## BOOKS

Athearn, Robert G. 1976. *The Coloradans.* Albuquerque: University of New Mexico Press 1985. *Glenwood Springs Centennial History.* Glenwood Springs: Tineagle Publishing

Bancroft, Caroline. 1958. *Glenwood's Early Glamour.* Boulder: Johnson Publishing Co.

Benson, Maxine. 1994. *1001 Colorado Place Names.* Lawrence: University Press of Kansas

Cassells, E. Steve. 1983. *The Archaeology of Colorado.* Boulder: Johnson Books

Ellis, Richard N. 1989. *The Ute Legacy.* Ignacio: Pinon Press

Goodwin, E.H., Duffy, Nellie, and Henderson, Jim. 1978. *Glenwood.* Glenwood Springs: Raymond The Printer

Gulliford, Andrew. 1983. *Garfield County, Colorado: The First Hundred Years 1883-1983.* Glenwood Springs: Gran Farnum Printing & Publishing Company

Haley, John L. 1994. *Wooing a Harsh Mistress: Glenwood Canyon's Highway Odyssey.* Greeley: Canyon Communications

Johnson, Anna and Yajko, Kathleen. 1983. *The Elusive Dream.* Glenwood Springs: Gran Farnum Printing & Publishing Company

Marsh, Charles S. 1982. *People of the Shining Mountains.* Boulder: Pruett

McGregor, Heather. 1992. *A Guide to Glenwood Canyon.* Glenwood Springs: Pika Publishing Co.

Myers, John Myers. 1955. *Doc Holliday.* Lincoln: University of Nebraska Press

Pettit, Jan. 1982. *Utes - The Mountain People.* Colorado Springs: Century One Press Publishing Company

Shoemaker, Len. 1973. *Roaring Fork Valley - An Illustrated Chronicle.* Sundance Publications, Limited

Traywick, Ben T. 1984. *Tombstone's Deadliest Gun: John Henry Holliday.* Red Marie's Books on the West

Urquart, Lena M. 1970. *Glenwood Springs: Spa in the Mountains.* Taylor Publishing Company

Werner, Fred H. 1985. *Meeker - The Story of the Meeker Massacre and Thornburgh Battle September 29, 1979.* Greeley: Werner Publications

**VIDEOTAPES**

*Highways & the Environment - Innovative Mitigation.* Viewfinder Productions, Inc., for the Federal Highway Commission

*I-70 - Where? How?.* 1972. Jerry Brown, Floyd Diemoz, Edward Mulhall, Jim Rose.

*Glenwood Canyon - Ancient Treasure, Modern Marvel.* 1993. Colorado Department of Transportation.

## ABOUT THE AUTHOR

I am, in real life, an accountant. My wife, Mary, and I have been fortunate enough to live in Glenwood Springs for the last 25 years. I have been active with the Chamber of Commerce, and am presently an adjunct member of the board of the Frontier Historical Society. Mary and I were also among the founding members of the Defiance Community Theater Company.

My previously published works include THE CASE OF THE BLUE CHICKEN, a satire of detective novels which has nothing whatsoever to do with history, I have also finished A QUICK HISTORY OF MARBLE AND REDSTONE. My second novel, a psychological fiction called COMPULSIVE, was published in September of 1998. A more complete history of Glenwood Springs will be published in 1999.

Many people assisted me in compiling this history and the accompanying photos. Janet Riley's knowledge and editorial skills were invaluable. Special thanks to Willa Soncarty and Ann Roberts of the Frontier Historical museum, as well as to the entire museum board. Thanks also to Sharon Graves, Don Vanderhoof, Floyd Diemonz, Bill Kight, Bill Shettig, Carlene Sampson, and Karen Holliday Tanner.

Jim Nelson